John Strecche, Canon of

the Life and Times of a Mediev

Geoffrey M. Hilton

2004

Kenilworth

First Published in 2004 by the Author,

G.M.Hilton,   28,Rouncil Lane,

Kenilworth, Warwickshire, CV8 1FF.

Obtainable from the address above

Printed and bound by
TW Printing Associates Ltd
Leamington Spa

ISBN 0 9536923 2 9

Incipit Liber Historiarum Sublimis Temporis Regum
Et sybillarum et annis Imperiis Omnium Regum

To my wife Hilary, for her enthusiastic support
throughout this venture

Contents

List of Figures, with Credits

I am most grateful to all those who have generously given their permission to use images for these illustrations.

Foreword

by Christopher de Hamel,
Donnelley Fellow Librarian,
Corpus Christi College, Cambridge.

To judge from the chronicle he wrote, John Strecche, Augustinian canon of Kenilworth, was probably a most agreeable man, for he had a good eye for the curious and amusing in his historical narrative, sometimes adding local references which must have delighted his medieval readers.

Strecche describes himself merely as *compilator*, a compiler rather than a writer. Dr Hilton himself stands in a direct line of historiographical descent from people like Strecche. He too is a compiler, with a flair for the utterly fascinating and bizarre little facts which bring history to life: on the supply of medieval shaving soap, the miseries of an army camping in the rain in northern England in 1327, on the body of Geoffrey de Clinton remaining uncorrupt and fragrant for two centuries, and on the possible wart on Strecche's nose. Medicine from Kenilworth Castle or Priory apparently cured the potentially deadly arrow wound on the face of the future King Henry V, a little local fact not generally known.

Like Strecche, Dr Hilton cannot gather enough information to fill his chronicle with absolute fact, to the great benefit of the reader, for both of them slip easily into anecdote and ancient legend. We learn here of Corineus hurling a giant off a cliff, of the thirty daughters of a King of Greece running riot in England rampant with lust, and of the ill-fated donkey Burnellus who travels to Salerno with a medical prescription for a new tail. This is a tradition of historical writing which goes back far into the

Middle Ages, mingling history with legends older than literacy and personal recollections of events.

John Strecche is not well known. This account takes us back to his troubled times, delighting in history: Strecche himself, if he could see it, would have approved mightily.

Christopher de Hamel,
Cambridge, August, 2004.

———————————————

Preface

This book is a journey back in time in search of the way of thinking and background influences of a medieval historian. It considers John Strecche in the context of his place and time: other books will be needed to transcribe and translate his writing about the Priors and their building works. Above all, it is hoped that this book will give another dimension to the ruins of the Abbey at Kenilworth for residents, visitors and students alike.

At the outset I have to admit that a great deal of the book is conjecture: we have only two manuscripts by John Strecche and we know only two dates in his later life, when he was Prior of Brooke. In the absence of any other evidence, I have optimistically supposed a biblical life-span of three score years and ten, from 1360 to 1430.

Reading the manuscript is not easy and the medieval writing must first be transcribed and then translated from Latin. I wish to thank especially Brian Jackson, Editor of the Magazine of Kenilworth History and Archaeology Society, with whom I have enjoyed many conversations about Strecche and his perplexing text, for allowing me to use some of his lively translations.

After some quotations I have added the Latin original: my hope is that English contains enough words of Latin origin to give a flavour of the way in which the quotations are expressed. This glorious language links a letter inviting a girl on Hadrian's Wall to a birthday party, the stories of the Anglo-Saxon monk Bede, the records of the Domesday Book, medieval chronicles, and the inscription on a 20th century pound coin - truly, an ornament and a safeguard, *decus et tutamen.*

The small superscript numbers in the text refer to the list of references at the back of the book. There are many references to folios in Strecche's manuscripts: in order not to clutter the text for the general reader these are given in a separate list and identified by chapter number and phrase.

I am greatly indebted to Norman Stevens and Harry Sunley, both for their comprehensive and erudite book *'Kenilworth, the Story of the Abbey'* and their willingness on many occasions to discuss their researches into the Abbey with me. A great deal of our knowledge about John Strecche and his Priory has only become evident at the beginning of the 21st century through the research and productions of the Abbey Interpretation Scheme. This remarkable work of collaboration receives due credit in the last Chapter.

I am very grateful to Norman Stevens for his meticulous examination of the final draft of this book, and to Terry Arnold and the staff of TW Printing who have taken the book into production.

My thanks are due to Dr de Hamel for his most generous Foreword, as vivid as the decoration in some of the medieval manuscripts which are his subjects for research.

Finally, I pay tribute to John Strecche, who has been a good companion during the time of writing this book.

Geoffrey Hilton,

Kenilworth,　August 2004.

———————————————

Chapter One. His achievements

The Augustinian Rule is more courteous than that of Benedict.
They go out when they like, mix with the world and talk at table [16]

John Strecche was a canon of the Augustinian Priory of St Mary, Kenilworth, Warwickshire. As a canon regular he was living by the rules of a monastery, but being an ordained priest he was able to say Mass and officiate in parish churches, unlike most monks at that time. Kenilworth Priory had a dependent cell, or outpost, in Rutland and Strecche was appointed Prior there in 1407, retiring in 1425. These are the only recorded dates in his life[40]. However, he was an author and writer, so from the manuscripts of his which survive, and our knowledge of Kenilworth Priory, this book ambitiously attempts to reconstruct his life. The Priory was raised to the status of Abbey about 1447, after his death: both terms may be used in this book.

If we suppose that he retired from Brooke in 1425, and we are optimistic that he lived the biblical three score years and ten, he could have been born in 1360, retired at the venerable age of 65, and died in 1430.

He has left two bound manuscripts which are substantially his own work: they are kept in the British Library in London[5]. His major work is a History of England starting rather obscurely with a history of Troy. The British Library description is 'A collection of romance and English history': it is much more coherent than this implies, as shown in Chapter Six. It includes chapters about the Priors of St Mary's Kenilworth and their building achievements and is of great interest to the people of Kenilworth and students of other priories. I will refer to this throughout the book as his 'History'. I will refer to the other work as his 'Miscellany'. We know so little about John Strecche that we have to make many assumptions about him from the threadbare evidence of the way in which he chose and wrote about his subjects.

Strecche is even modest about disclosing his own name, perhaps as an exercise in humility: however, he does leave several clues to it. He draws a large monogram to act as the title page, below which is an acrostic couplet spelling *Ion Strecche*. An explanatory statement about authorship, colophon, at the end of the Third Book directs readers to another acrostic, the initial letter of each Chapter of the first three books spelling *Iohannes Strecche Canonicus* (Appendix). However, following the History of Troy by Guido delle Colonne, Strecche prints his name in a cheerfully careless box *I Strecche*. He also writes, in his Miscellany, a penitentiary colophon

> Have pity on thy servant John Strecche, protecting him with thy mantle

> *Involvens pannis puerum miserere Iohannis Strecche*

and he uses his Christian name in a devotional ending to his poem on Henry V

> Now to him be honour and glory and everlasting praise

> Whose divine law and love grow in the mind of John

> *Ipse nunc sit honor et gloria, lausque perhennis*

> *Cuius fas et amor crescat in mente Iohannis*

Strecche loved poetry. He begins and ends his History with verse and uses it in praise of the characters in whom he is most interested and perhaps with whom he hopes to inspire his readers. His Miscellany includes a five-page treatise on different kinds of verse.

The name Strecche seems to be an older form of the word 'stretch' with a superfluous *c* rather than *t*: this form occurs in Chaucer's Pardoner's Tale: 'Thanne peyne I me to strecche forth the nekke'. The surname occurs in many medieval documents, for example 'Robert Strecche alias Strech, sometimes the King's forester, held one virgate of land from the Prior of Kenilworth'[39]. A Streche family member was a 17th century benefactor of Wareham, and another has given his name to a street in Swanage.

What did he look like? This might seem an absurd question since he lived such a long time ago, and was not famous even in his lifetime. He would have had a monastic tonsure, a fringe of hair round a shaven bald pate, and probably the beard that Augustinians were allowed to grow. But it could be that we are fortunate enough to have a cartoon of him! In the early 15th century, manuscripts were frequently defaced with marginal drawings. These started as cuffed hands with fingers pointing to significant texts, perhaps those which had to be learnt by heart, but became elaborated into sketches by bored readers. Animal heads were common and then human faces. In the margin of a page in his Miscellany it is just possible that one of his students has drawn his master: the bearded canon, with a wart on his nose.

The sense of Strecche being a teacher of novices in the Priory comes across very strongly. Much of the work is hurriedly written and elegance is sacrificed for rapidity. It is heavily abbreviated, suggesting a manuscript originally written for immediate use rather than posterity. It gives the impression of a book compiled for use within the Priory, possibly for the instruction of novices or for reference by canons. This impression is strengthened by the words of the acrostic on the title page (see Frontispiece) in which Strecche thanks his Prior, Thomas Kidderminster, for asking him to write the book. The words are feint but likely to have the sense

Our work makes known our distinguished times.

Beloved lord (Prior) you have graciously desired this from (me)

Indicat Opus Nostrum Sublimia Tempora

Regum Excellene Carum Cupiens Hanc Ex.

Were his times sublime? England had recovered from the outbreaks of plague during the reign of Edward III, and the troublesome period at the end of the reign of Richard II: heresy had been expunged by the burning of Lollards, and a measure of prosperity followed the plundering of France by Henry V. If he was writing in 1407, there had been a succession of seven good harvests[36]. The Time Chart at the end of this chapter includes some events which we generally regard as significant.

The text of his History of England is analysed in detail in the Appendix. From the arrival of the Anglo-Saxons to the death of King Henry IV, it is divided conveniently into chapters, usually one or more for each reign, and later one for each Prior. In the first three books the chapter length is dictated to some extent by the need for a suitable acrostic letter.

Book Four, from William I to Richard II, is essentially a record of dates and basic facts for each reign, being precise about the age and year of reign of the monarchs, and above all validating their reign by naming the Archbishop conducting the coronation and frequently the Pope, and excessive repetition of royal ancestries. Strecche is more concerned with the deeds of the monarch and his mode of death and burial than with the events of his reign. C.L.Kingsford, who was the first 20th century historian to write about Strecche[32], goes so far as to say the Latin style is bad and from a literary point of view worthless, though neither he nor subsequent authors have recognised the many passages which come from a chronicle - to be revealed later - which I am certain is his major source. However, the bald narrative is relieved by occasional verses, which are announced with a flourish, eg: 'the author writes the following verse - *compilator metrice sic scripsit*'. The inclusion of these verses seems an attractive way of enlivening the text while inculcating special regard for the Priory and the King of the Realm. As a teacher, he is meticulous about authenticating dates of events. For example, the burial of Prior Robert Salle was 'in the year of grace 1312, the fifth year of the reign of King Edward II, son of Edward I, in the pontificate of Pope Clement V' - and part of this is repeated on the next page. The manuscript is even bound with fragments of a calendar from which he could plan a series of lessons. The letters b - g suggest a six-day secular week, omitting A, Sunday, when religious observance would preclude

Fig.1b.

Fig.1a. A canon of the Augustinian Order (black canon). A black cope, or
cloak with hood, lies over a white linen rochet with tight sleeves, over a
black woollen cassock, lined with lambskins in winter. (After Dugdale,
Monasticon Anglicum)

Fig.1b. 15th century cartoon of a canon with a wart on his nose, drawn in
the margin of fo.87v, Manuscript 38665

study, as would the Saint's day marked. These letters for days of the week still appear in the Anglican Book of Common Prayer.

The whole nature of the text changes in the second part of Book Five, however, dealing with the reign of Henry V. Strecche was living close to Kenilworth Castle, where King Henry spent a good deal of time, and he was able to enrich his accounts of contemporary events with gossip from the castle. The contrast between the two Books is well illustrated by three comments by A.Gransden[14], which must be based on Book Five Henry V: 'Strecche has little on the Priory's domestic history, he is not pious, he is fascinated by warfare'. None of these comments can be justified for Book Four. In fifty-one chapters of Book Four, from William I to Richard II, there are 1099 lines: of these, 386, 35%, are Priory History. In ten chapters of Book Five Henry IV, there are 227 lines: of these, 59, 26%, are Priory History. On the other hand, less than 5% of Book Five Henry V is Priory History. As will be seen later, it is certainly not fair to accuse him of lack of piety, even in Book Five.

Strecche clearly has the tradition of the Priory as a unique source for some of his works[24] and, in the time of Henry V, the advantage of being on the spot in Kenilworth where, as a Prince, Henry was treated in 1403 after the battle of Shrewsbury. He revisited as King, on at least four more occasions, *castellum suum dilectum de Kennilleworth*. Unfortunately Strecche has little to say about the Siege of Kenilworth, 1266, which was the longest siege in English medieval history and of national significance, in his chapter about Prior Wilfred, although he may have related more in Chapter 28, which is missing. For historical facts, he must have relied on copies of the writings of other chronicles that circulated round the monasteries or which he could have encountered when he trained for ordination.

Where might Strecche have studied for the priesthood? He may have been sent to Oxford under the quota system demanded by Pope Benedict's Statute for the Education of Monks, 1336. This required Houses to send to University, and provide with a yearly pension, one in twenty of their number fit to acquire the fruit of greater learning and pass it on. If he was sent there, he was lucky: in 1443 the Prior and Convent of Kenilworth were fined twenty pounds for failing to send anyone to University for the previous two years[40]. At Oxford was the Augustinian Priory of St Frideswide (later to become Christchurch College and Cathedral), where he may have lodged: the Augustinian College of St Mary was not founded until after 1435. At the University he would have been exposed to the juxtaposition of Classical profanity and Christian piety which fortunately made the monasteries, and the Universities modelled upon them, repositories of our knowledge of the art and science of the Greeks and Romans. He would have learnt about the Classical authors, to whom he makes reference (see the Fable of Albina). Chaucer mocks the overenthusiastic use of such references by giving the earthy stories of his pilgrims this patina of respectability. But citation of the Classical authors was a necessary adjunct of Rhetoric and hence History. This foreshadows the modern use of textual references: then, as now, one might not have actually read the references in order to be able to cite them!

Strecche is careful to describe himself as *compilator* rather than *scriptor,* although in fact a considerable part of his Fourth Book is about Kenilworth Priory and likely to be his own work. The emphasis on the continuity and validity of the Establishment, the comparative paucity of important events in English history, and the details of the Priors of Kenilworth and their achievements, proclaim this History to be one for the particular needs of St Mary's Priory. In this it has been successful, and John Strecche has increased the reputation of the House by establishing its antiquity, and proclaiming the generosity, saintliness and nobility of its benefactors, even into the twenty-first century.

TIME CHART FOR THE LIFE AND TIMES OF
JOHN STRECCHE

1337 EDWARD III claims the French throne and declares war on France: the Hundred Years' War (to 1453)

1348 -50 The Black Death, First Plague

1352 Ranulph Higden finishes writing his *Polychronicon*

ca.1360 John Strecche born?

1361 Second Plague: Prior Peyto and 17 canons of Kenilworth Priory die

1362 English replaces French for legislation

1374-5 Third Plague outbreak

1377 RICHARD II accedes to the throne

1380 John Wycliffe translates the New Testament into English

1381 The Peasants' Revolt against the Poll Tax

1398 Geoffrey Chaucer finishes the Canterbury Tales

1399 HENRY IV usurps the throne

1401 Lollards, followers of John Wycliffe, burned for heresy

1403 The future King Henry V severely injured in the face at the Battle of Shrewsbury and brought to Kenilworth for treatment to his wound

1407 John Strecche appointed Prior of Brooke

1413 HENRY V accedes to the throne

1415 Henry renews the claim to the French throne and wins the Battle of Agincourt

1422 HENRY VI accedes to the throne.

1425 John Strecche retires as Prior of Brooke

ca.1430 John Strecche died?

1431 Joan of Arc burned at the stake

ca.1447 St Mary's Priory Kenilworth raised to status of Abbey

1477 William Caxton establishes his Printing Press at Westminster

8

Chapter Two. His life in the Priory

It is good for us to be here, where man lives more purely, falls more rarely, rises more speedily and proceeds more surely [46]

When Geoffrey de Clinton, Chamberlain and Treasurer to King Henry I, was granted land in Kenilworth, he used some for a Castle, and some for a Priory. Strecche records the founding of the Priory in a celebratory verse in Book Five and this is presumably the most accurate date for foundation we have, although most religious house wrote Chronicles with the intention of enhancing their antiquity as much as they dared. I am grateful to Brian Jackson[28] for the following translations of Strecche's verse and text:

> In the year 1119, when the great Henry the First was King of England, then did Geoffrey de Clinton establish this place with pious gifts - in the name of the Virgin he founded this place to be sacred to the Mother of Christ - he founded a Priory pleasing to himself where he desired canons to be servants of Christ - he laid it down that they should be lavishly funded - this worthy knight ordered costly grants, which the King indeed as an act of piety increased. Then, forestalled by death, the knight sought his place in heaven and was entombed with all praise here in the Priory. Thus he lay for more than two hundred years.. In the tomb he remained fragrant and free from corruption - untouched by decay so that, sanctified by Christ, he remained an intact and unsullied corpse. Both his son and grandson are also here interred.

On the site in Kenilworth, in The Barn Museum, there is a stone coffin taken from the Chapter House during the 1922-23 excavations. It is possible that this was for one of the Founders mentioned in this verse. There is a drainage hole in the base of it, which would have facilitated drying of the corpse rather than decay and corruption: freedom from decay was a badge of saintliness. (The stone recess for a Prior's crozier introduces some doubt about its being a Founder's tomb: on the other hand, Founders in some other Houses are known to have been considered to be honorary Priors or Abbots).

The verse above was written as a result of the opening and restoration of the tombs of the Founders, which Strecche is likely to have been recalled from Brooke to witness, as the text preceding the verse shows (Primary Source 2):

Concerning Tombs and Effigies of the Founders:

And in that same fourth year of the reign of King Henry V, the year of Our Lord 1417, Johannes Mukelton, the cellarer to the sub-prior and the House, undertook completely to restore, decorate and paint the tombs of the Founders in the Chapter House of Kenilworth Priory.

Now when the wooden tomb, which stood above the sepulchres of the said Founders had been removed, there appeared three marble slabs. From these, certain people from the Priory lifted the middle stone, under which Geoffrey de Clinton lay entire in his fragrant tomb.

When they had seen and touched him, the said stone was replaced as it had been at first. And they painted the said tombs with the images of the Founders, with all due reverence, so that they might contemplate them face to face in that same place.

The Priory was primarily for the function of having Masses said for the Founders' souls in perpetuity. Priories were expensive to found: besides land for their buildings, gardens and fields, they needed estates whose tenants could produce special items such as beeswax for the church candles, serve as labourers in the fields and pay rent. The full force of religious belief could be brought to bear on these tenants to fulfil their duties. A charter of

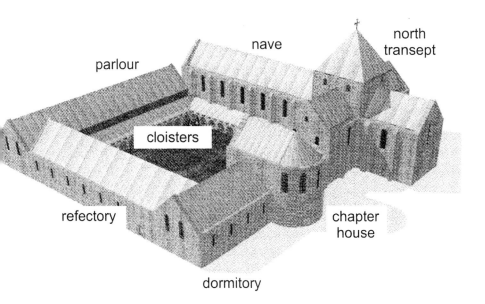

parlour

nave

north transept

cloisters

refectory

chapter house

dormitory

ig.2a. Reconstruction of Kenilworth Priory as it may have looked at the end of
the 13th century.
The Gatehouse would be built to the west (top left) and the infirmary and
monastic garden to the east (bottom right).

ig.2b. Silver coins of King Richard II (1377-1399):
Groat (4d) obverse: RICARD D GRA REX ANGLIE +
with King's face, hardly changing from Edward I to Henry VII.
Half-groat reverse: POSUI DEUM ADIUTOREM MEUM
I have made God my helper (Psalm 54,v.4), with lines to serve as guides for
cutting, ending in serifs to restrict illegal clipping.
Silver penny: Inscribed as above.
They might buy: 4d.a pair of boots,2d.a goose,1d.two dozen eggs

Henry III [5,18] confirms that Walter de Bays must bring six pence a year for the sustenance of the canons to be placed before the image of the Virgin Mary by the great altar in their church - *Ego Walter de Bays confirmam canonices de Kenell sex denarii annui redditus ad sustentam commune isdem terei coram imagine Beate Marie ad magnum altarum in ecclesia conventuali eorum.* Who would dare to cheat or fail with such a bailiff!

Geoffrey de Clinton's Foundation was an expression of of piety and remorse for wrongdoing. The responsibility of maintaining perpetual prayer and Masses for him and his co-founders was taken very seriously and Strecche honours their memory in his text and verses. He was fortunately not to know that that this was to be brought to an end by the greed of Henry VIII and his ministers. The Founders devoutly believed in the doctrine of praying for the souls of the dead and it seems hard that their wishes have been frustrated and they must be content with Masses on All Souls' Day in the Catholic tradition. However, their fears and their piety resulted in the creation of Priories and Abbeys, which were beacons of charity and learning for cruel and uncivilised times.

However, Geoffrey economised to a degree by founding, not a monastery of monks, but a priory of Augustinian canons who were ordained priests and able to bring income to the priory from churches to which they were appointed. Kenilworth Castle was a royal castle and many of the Kings of England visited it. While there, they would go to worship in the Priory and would make presents to it which they expected to qualify them as further Founders deserving perpetual prayer: Henry VIII did this shortly before dissolving his Foundation!

The life of a canon was governed by the spiritual life of the Priory, built around the eight offices: Matins and Lauds at midnight, Prime at daybreak, Terce, Sext, Nones, Vespers, and finally Compline at about sunset. In addition there were Masses, private Masses (often for benefactors), private devotion, and processions of the convent. This was a punishing routine, recognised as the *tedium claustrum*. There would inevitably be strained relationships and personality clashes in the closed community, mischievously imagined by Robert Browning[7] ('Primary Source' 3). The whole convent met daily in the Chapter House for a reading from the Rule of Saint Augustine, attention to business and discipline, including corporal punishment.

Other activities had to be fitted in between. Details of a canon's daily life are recorded in a book of Observances, or customs, dated 1296 which has survived from Barnwell Priory, Cambridge[8] (transcription and translation by J.W.Clarke).

Silence was enjoined at fixed hours and places: the church, the dormitory, the cloister until after Chapter, and the refectory, except with guests. The rules could be broken in the event of robbery, sickness, outbreak of fire, overseeing workmen, and receiving princes of the church or state. Seemly talking was permitted in the parlour. The spiritual life of the canons was rigorous and the punishments for transgressions, meted out in the Chapter House, were severe. In contrast, the canons were very well looked after physically by the standards of the time. Clean freshwater came from a culverted spring and waste was drained rapidly to a flowing brook. Kings staying in nearby Kenilworth Castle were glad to visit the cleaner and more comfortable Priory, where there would be special guest quarters and good food at the Prior's table. John of Gaunt even had a dance floor erected in the Priory[40].

The canons were surrounded by glorious, vividly coloured architecture, and art, and music and literature, and they had gardens and orchards to walk in. They were given servants, regular meals, security, hygiene, medicine and education far in excess of the nobles in their Castles. Unfortunately, the labourers who created and paid tithes for all this were excluded, only the destitute receiving some charity at the Gatehouse or in the Almonry. Had the Abbeys been willing to share their wealth there might have been many more Pilgrimages of Grace to deter King Henry and Thomas Cromwell from their devastating actions.

It was the duty of the Fraterer to provide canons with clean salt, washed cups and spoons (they carried their own knives), jugs of freshly drawn beer, and bread that is clean, not burnt nor gnawed by mice nor soiled - *panes sint mundi non adusti nec a muribus corrosi vel sordido.* Augustinians were allowed meat and the canons were allowed to fish in the Castle mere on Thursdays, as well as having their own pool. The Chamberlain was to provide warm water and soap for shaving (though they retained neat beards), and baths if asked for. Their clothes, which were linen, were to be washed every fortnight in summer, by a laundress of good reputation, who must also do the mending. A tailor was to visit and fit the clothes properly. They wore a long sheepskin-lined black cassock and black (later blue) cloaks when outside the monastery.

The medical services were the best available at the time. The Master of the Infirmary was to be compassionate and always to have ginger, cinnamon and peony to hand. He should summon a physician when necessary and permit the seriously ill to eat, drink, talk and sleep when they will. In an age when blood-letting was at the fore-front of good - and expensive - medical practice, brethren could request to be bled as often as every seven weeks. For three days afterwards they should live a life of comfort and happiness in the Infirmary, though they must not annoy each other with sarcastic language, or play dice or chess.

In a show of democracy, rare for medieval times, the Priors were elected by the Canons: *in priorem electus et installatus fuit* - but for Prior Kidderminster, under whom Strecche served, he adds 'God be praised'.

Many servants were employed: Kenilworth had 16 - 20 canons and a total establishment of 70 - 87, including servants, farm workers and pensioners (corrodians).   The Barnwell Observances prescribe for the control of servants and attempt to limit their contact with canons. In the dormitory, if occasionally women are admitted, care must be taken that they are of good repute, not admitted without many witnesses, and without delay sent forth - *si aliquando mulieres introducantur considerandum est quod sint bone fame et sine testimonio plurium non introducantur et sine mora reducantur.*

Fig.3. The Chapter House, Bristol Cathedral, formerly an Augustinian Abbey. Completed 1165 A.D., it is one of the finest Norman rooms in existence. The walls are lined with blind arcading and the roof is supported by vaulting ribs ornamented with chevron moulding. Kenilworth Chapter House would have been very similar, though slightly larger[40]: samples of its ribs and arcading have been reconstructed from the original stones and placed in The Barn exhibition. *Photograph by Philippa Johnson*

It is possible that some of these observances may have been less honoured by 1400, especially in view of the acerbic comments Chaucer makes about his religious characters. Chaucer was in the service of John of Gaunt and he sent twenty masons to the Castle in 1392 to assist in the rebuilding of the Great Hall[27]. Brian Jackson speculates that, in view of their long personal relationship and connection through marriage, Chaucer could have visited the Castle and hence the Priory, where John of Gaunt kept special rooms. Here he would encounter the Black Canons - and even Strecche among them. The repeated insistence that canons should be present at all the services, and joining in all the processions, rather implies that sometimes they were not. Many of the observances make allowance for those who are late. Strecche may have received special leave from his Prior to write and this may be the reason for his acrostic which thanks his Prior for desiring the work from him. He may also have found more freedom while he was Prior of Brooke.

Chapter Three. Chronicles and Histories

The splendour of historical writing is to be cherished with the greatest delight[15]

John Strecche introduces the various books of his manuscript as histories, but they bear more of the characteristics of medieval chronicles.

A chronicle is history in the form of accounts of dated events, originally without discussion of their significance. The most famous is the Anglo-Saxon Chronicle which starts by recounting events in pre-Roman Britain and is continued in a complex series of manuscripts until a century after the Battle of Hastings. Chronicles written for education in the monasteries and universities were in Latin prose, often with verses in elegiac or heroic metre. French verse was favoured for Court circles and English verse for the entertainment of the merchant class, verse being easier to memorise and listen to.

The most popular of medieval English chronicles were known as 'Brut' e.g. Castleford's *The boke of Brut*. This name was derived from the legend of Brutus, fictional first prince of Britain, as claimed by Geoffrey of Monmouth. A French prose original summarised Geoffrey's history, then added a more sober account of events up to the time of writing, Edward I. Translated into English and Latin, *The Brut* survives in 200 manuscripts and Caxton's chronicles. *Roman de Brut* by Robert Wace, Norman court poet for Henry II, was a version of Geoffrey of Monmouth in Anglo-Norman verse, about1155, being the first to add the Round Table to the King Arthur story, and the basis of Lawman's version. Lawman's - or Layamon's - Middle English verse *Brut*, about 1200, reworked Geoffrey's account, closely based on the *Roman de Brut*. The most comprehensive chronicle was *Polychronicon*, a

Latin History of the World to about 1364 by Ranulph Higden, a monk of Chester Abbey[33]. It was eventually translated into quaint English by John Trevisa, Vicar of Berkeley 1342-1402, then printed by Caxton and became the most popular account of English history until Walter Raleigh's. Higden was accused of being an arrant plagiarist of Roger of Chester. This charge seems rather unfair since a monk had little opportunity for independent research and most of the monastic chronicles were the product of an exchange of manuscripts: Strecche records lending books to 'dominus Joh. Susex, dom. Petrus de Preston, Will. Clerke de Okam'.

Some chroniclers were relating their own experiences and were medieval journalists. Jean Le Bel fought with King Edward III's army in Scotland in 1327 and was quoted by Jean Froissart (translation of G.Brereton)[4]:

> The battalions began to move forward at daybreak, over heaths, hills and valleys and through difficult woodland, without a trace of level country. Among the mountains and valleys were great marshes and bogs, and anyone who got stuck in them was left, never to be seen again: they rode hard, with no halts except to piss and retighten their horses' girths. By late afternoon, young King Edward and his army reached the Tyne: exhausted by the day's journey, they forded it with great difficulty owing to the great stones which lay in it. When they gained the other side, each chose a piece of ground along the bank on which to spend the night. They had to sleep in full armour, holding their horses by the bridles since they had nothing to tie them to: few of them had axes to cut wood and build shelters. They had nothing to eat all that day and night, except the loaves which they had tied behind their saddles, and these were all soiled and sodden with the horses' sweat. Then it began to rain.

Many medieval chronicles were written in monasteries which give their names to the chronicle and recorded events in the life of the House. Some were lists of events without comment, but

Fig.4a. Canon's Choir Stall
in St Mary's Church,
Halford, Warwickshire,
reputed to come from
Kenilworth Abbey[44].

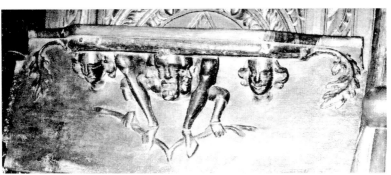

Fig.4b. Raised seat to show the misericord of the stall, with the figure of a tumbler
(three faces), two heads and two oak leaves. The species is, unusually, sessile
oak: pedunculate oak was most commonly carved in medieval times. Oak had
pagan connotations and was best hidden under the seat.

others extended into the realms of true histories. Ranulph Higden gave this not too flattering portrayal of King Henry II (16th century translation):

> Kynge Henry was a corpulent man with yelowe eien and a grete voice, of a mean stature, eloquente and litterate, more manly and courteous towards a dead knight than one being in life. This kynge was a voluntary transgressor of his word and promise, an open spousebreker, unkynde alle tymes to God, and luffynge discorde between his childer.

The true historians demonstrated powers of selection, imagination and synthesis which distinguished them from the chroniclers. History was regarded as a form of rhetoric and was expected to include references to the ancient philosophers, poetry, impersonations of orations by the princes and prelates who played their parts in it, portraits of their characters, and moralistic commentaries on their behaviour.

History's finest practitioner was Henry, Archdeacon of Huntingdon[1,15]. He said:

History brings the past into view as though it were the present, and allows judgment of the future by representing the past.

Historia igitur praeterita quasi presentia visui representat, futura ex praeteritis imaginando dijudicat

and he wrote in his epilogue of 1135:

> Now I speak to you who will be living in the third Millennium, about the 135th year. I, who will already be dust by your time, have made mention of you in this book, so long before you are to be born, so that if this book comes into your hands, I beg you to pray for me, poor wretch.

He writes a long oration for Duke William at Hastings, finishing:

> 'Raise your standards, men, and let there be no moderation to your righteous anger. Let the lightning of your glory be

seen from the east to the west, let the thunder of your charge be heard, and may you be the avengers of most noble blood'. William had not yet concluded his speech, when all his men, boiling with unbelievable anger, charged forward in their lines with indescribable force against the enemy - and left the Duke alone, speaking to himself.

John Strecche can be considered as writing a chronicle, but he gives the vestiges of a rhetorical approach in the inclusion of verses celebrating, or summing up the lives, characters and achievements of a King or a Prior, and his fable of Albina cites the ancient philosophers, and ends moralistically.

The main source of Strecche's Chronicle up to the reign of Edward III was undoubtedly Ranulph Higden's *Polychronicon*. On page after page, sentences are identical in the two works. Of 433 lines concerning national history, I have so far identified 112, 26%, as being direct quotations from Higden. In the earlier Books even more is owed to Higden: for example, 73% of the text for Harold Harefoot and Harthacanute. The following eulogy for Edward II, which he copied word for word from Higden, does not seem to be the most pertinent one to use in a précis but he may have decided that it would be memorable for his students.

At the beginning of his reign, the earth yielded much fruit, the air was temperate, the sea tranquil and the church free

In cuius primordiis grata suggebantur auspicia nam et tunc terra recepit ubertatem aer temperiem mare tranquillitatem ecclesia libertatem.

In his short chapter on Richard I, he selects from Higden

The manners and acts of whom Stephen of Canterbury describes clearly

Cuius mores et actus Stephanus Cantuariensis luculentur descripsit.

This seems redundant unless, of course, it is a reference given to send students off to the book cupboard. However, Strecche is careful in his selection of Higden's text and does not repeat

Higden's description of the eldest son of Edward III as Edward IV, knowing him as the Black Prince who predeceased his father. When copying from Higden, his handwriting becomes more hurried and his use of abbreviations increases. The most convincing evidence for his reliance on this source comes at the end of Chapter 38, (Fig.10a) where he indirectly acknowledges his debt to Ranulph Higden:

> Ranulph of Chester finished his work and awaited the fate of death

> *Et Ranulphus Cestrensis hic opus suis finuit et fatum mortem aspexit.*

He omits most of Higden's colourful stories, but cannot resist the tale against William I, whose burial plot had to be bought for £100 from a wronged Knight. Throughout Book Four, Strecche refers to the Norman Conquest in fixing the dates of the reigns of Kings: at the end, he puts in a final - and it is tempting to say pejorative - William the Bastard.

Strecche may have read the chronicler of Dieulacres Abbey, Staffordshire[13], writing about the Battle of Shrewsbury, where Prince Henry, later to become King Henry V, was fighting for his father:

> Henry, then a boy hardly aged sixteen, was severely wounded in the face near the nose by an arrow: by the grace of God he recovered

> *Henricus tunc puer quasi XVI annorum graviter vulneratus est in facie cum sagitta prope narum: dei gracia convaluit*

But Strecche added to this (Fig.10c), from his own knowledge,

> who after the battle was brought to the Castle of Kenilworth with his injury and there cured by the art of medicine

> *qui post bellum cum suis lesis ad castrum Kenill veniens ibidem curatus erat per artem medicine*

The arrow penetrated the young Prince's cheek, with the arrowhead

Fig.5. The canons' garden of Haverfordwest Augustinian Priory, Pembrokeshire.
The rectangular raised beds have stone foundations, possibly with additional timber boards.
Amongst them is an exhedra, turf seat, representing the Virgin's womb, with the Christchild in the centre.
Excavation and reconstruction by Dr Sian E. Rees of CADW.

The site of the canons' garden at Kenilworth is not known but might be revealed by geophysical techniques.

becoming embedded in the back of the skull. It is astonishing that the arrowhead was extracted by the skillful surgery of John Bradmore[2], and even more amazing that sepsis did not set in (Primary Source 1). It is highly likely that the medicine would be practised by a physician assisted by a canon of St Mary's Priory, using herbs grown in the Priory garden.

Strecche was cited, though spelt Strench, as an authority alongside Giraldus Cambrensis, by John Rous in his *History of Kings of England* [21] circa 1485. King Athelstan was represented in a fight by Collibrandus 'a man of immense stature'. Strecche merely says 'a giant' but since the great historian William of Malmesbury does not mention Collibrandus at all, Rous feels the need for support for his statement. Rous was chaplain at the chapel of St.Mary Magdalen at Guy's Cliffe, Warwick, a four mile walk to Kenilworth Priory, by tracks which still exist as local footpaths. He could have met an aged Strecche, or at least consulted his library.

Strecche was in the tradition of the monastic chronicle, though he does not match the standards of presentation, and historical comment, of chroniclers of earlier centuries[14].

Chapter Four. The Legend of Brutus

The soothsayers said this boy, after he had wandered through many lands, would rise to the highest honour[43]

Many of the medieval chroniclers, including Strecche himself, attempted to explain how Britain came to be populated and the origin of its name. William of Malmesbury is content to start with the Roman Occupation [37] and the most straightforward of the writers is one of the earliest, the Venerable Bede of the monastery of St Peter at Jarrow [34]. His book 'History of the English Church and People', 731, begins 'Britain, formerly known as Albion, is an island in the ocean. At the present time there are four nations, English, British (Welsh), Scots (Irish) and Picts. At first the only inhabitants were Britons, from whom it takes its name, and who, according to tradition, crossed into Britain from Armorica (Brittany).'

By the beginning of the 12th century these simple ideas had been elaborated into the legend of Brutus, great-grandson of Aeneas of Troy, and these trojanising notions held our chroniclers in thrall. A major source for this legend is Geoffrey of Monmouth, who completed his *History of the Kings of Britain* in 1136. He based some of it on Nennius' *Historia Brittonum*. The following account of the legend consists of extracts from the writing of Geoffrey of Monmouth himself[43], translated by Lewis Thorpe:

> After the Trojan war, Aeneas fled from the ruined city with his son Ascanius and came by boat to Italy. He was honourably received there by King Latinus but attacked by King Turnus, whom he killed. He married Lavinia and their son Ascanius fathered Silvius, who fathered Brutus, the great-

grandson of Aeneas. Brutus accidentally killed his father and was expelled from Italy, to wander round the Mediterranean with a band of Trojan exiles. After many feats of bravery, he came to a temple of Diana. He poured libations before her statue and spoke these words: 'O powerful goddess, terror of the forest glades, yet hope of the wild woodlands, tell me of a safe dwelling place where I am to worship you down the ages, and where, to the chanting of maidens, I shall dedicate temples to you.' This he said nine times, then fell into a sleep. Then the goddess Diana appeared to him in a dream and spoke these words: 'Brutus, beyond the setting of the sun, past the realms of Gaul, there lies an island in the sea once occupied by giants. Now it is empty and ready for your folk. Down the years this will prove an abode suited to you and your people, and for your descendants it will be a second Troy. A race of kings will be born there from your stock and the whole earth will be subject to them.

Thus encouraged, the Trojans passed through the Pillars of Hercules and, after many exploits in France, joined with Corineus, another exile leader, and with the winds behind them sought the promised isle and finally landed at Totnes. At this time the island of Britain was called Albion and was uninhabited except for a few giants. It was, however, most attractive because of the delightful situation of its regions, its forests and its many rivers which teemed with fish. They drove the giants whom they had discovered into caves in the mountains and divided the land amongst themselves. Brutus then called the island Britain and his companions Britons. His intention was that his memory should be perpetuated by the derivation of the name.

Corineus, however, following in this the example of his leader, called the region which had fallen to his share Cornwall. He experienced great pleasure from wrestling with the giants, of whom there were far more there than in any other region. Among them was a particularly repulsive one called Gogmagog who was twelve feet tall. He was so strong that he could tear up an oak tree as if it were a hazel wand. Corineus challenged him to a wrestling match. The contest began and each of them caught the other in a hold by twining his arms around him and the air vibrated with their panting breath. Gogmagog gripped Corineus with all his might and broke three of his ribs, two on the right side and one on the left. Corineus then summoned all his strength, for he was infuriated by what had happened. He heaved Gogmagog up on to his shoulders and, running as fast as he could under the weight, he hurried off to the nearby coast. He clambered up to the top of a mighty cliff, shook himself free and hurled this deadly monster, whom he was carrying on his shoulders, far out into the sea. The giant fell on to a sharp reef of rocks, where he was dashed into a thousand fragments and stained the waters with his blood. The place is called Gogmagog's Leap to this day.

Once he had divided up his kingdom, Brutus decided to build a capital. He came at length to the river Thames and chose a site there, calling the city Troia Nova: by corruption of the words it became Trinovantum. At that time the priest Eli was ruling in Judea.

Brutus had three sons by Ignoge. When he died, they divided the kingdom between them. Locrinus inherited the part afterwards called Loegria, after him. Kamber received the region which is on the further bank of the River Severn, now known as Wales, but for a long time called Kambria from his name. As a result, the people of that country still call themselves Kambri in the Welsh tongue. Albanectus took the region which is now called Scotland: he called it Albany, after his own name.

The reference to the priest Eli would date these events at about 1100 B.C. After writing about the Romans, Merlin, King Arthur and Cadwallader, Geoffrey finishes his history with Saxon domination of the British, which he attributes to God's punishment for their degeneracy, a judgement by which some chroniclers later justify the Norman Conquest of the degenerate Anglo-Saxons.

In an early attempt at copyright, Geoffrey recommends other chroniclers to say nothing at all about the kings of the Britons, since they do not have in their possession 'the book in the British language which Walter Archdeacon of Oxford brought from Wales. It is this book I have been at such pains to translate into Latin in this way' - *librum illum britannicis sermonis quem Walterus oxfordensis archidiaconis ex britannia adnexit quidem historia hoc modem latinum sermonem transferre curavi*. Strecche takes this to heart and for his own history gets his pupil John Aston to copy Geoffrey's work faithfully, including the copyright warning.

William of Newburg, ca. 1135 - 1198, an Augustinian from Yorkshire, wrote a history of English affairs from the Norman Conquest, *Historia Rerum Anglicarum*, denouncing Geoffrey as a writer of fiction not history: 'A writer in our time has started up and invented the most ridiculous fictions concerning the Britons'. Nevertheless, the legend was taken up with enthusiasm and rewritten in every possible way. The author of Sir Gawain and the Green Knight uniquely gives Brutus the prename Felix: however, 'happy' was an epithet customarily used in the Roman tradition for the founders of cities. The Elizabethan poets wrote about him (Michael Drayton[10] in *Polyolbion*, Edmund Spenser in *The Fairie Queene*) and William Blake writes of 'the triple-headed Gog-Magog of Albion'. Totnes displays its Brutus Stone on the north side of Fore Street: the hero is said to have put his foot upon the stone when he came ashore, declaring boldly 'Here I stand and here I rest: this good town shall be called Totnes'. London also has its Brutus stone (at 111, Cannon Street).

Gogmagog persists in folklore and some place-names. The lofty heights of 222 feet east of Cambridge are called the Gog Magog Hills, and Gog Brook by Warwick racecourse is said to have been straightened by a giant. Near Tiverton lie the hamlets of Gogland and Gogwell. At some point the giant underwent binary fission, so that Gog and Magog stand as nine-foot (fifteen-foot until 1940) figures in London's Guildhall.

It is difficult to know just how much Strecche believed in this legend. As a pious Christian he could hardly have believed that

Fig.6. Illuminated word 'Albion' at the opening of a 9th century copy of Bede's *History of the English Church and People*, A.D. 731. The name is possibly derived from the white cliffs that faced the Roman invaders.

The lines read:

INSULA CUI QUONDAM   ALBION NOMEN FUIT
an island to which formerly   the name Albion was given

The scribe has embellished the opening words of his copy by decorating the terminals of many of the letters. There is a menagerie of beasts, having horns, crests, long tongues (one knotted), long ears and interlaced boneless bodies. They bite anything they can get their jaws round, egged on by a mischievous Green Man.

the goddess Diana spoke to Brutus. On the other hand, he was sufficiently interested in the Trojans to have introduced his chronicle by copying out himself verses about the fall of Troy. Then he had copied for him, firstly, a 130 page history of Troy by Guido delle Colonne, and secondly, Geoffrey of Monmouth, the whole of the first book of which is concerned with the Brutus legend. Between all these, he writes five short notes on Brutus, and complains that Troy was only conquered by trickery. No doubt it was important to him that Rome and Britain shared the same ancestry of Aeneas and Troy, and came to adopt the same Christian faith.

Chapter Five. The Fable of Albina

They brought forth Geaunts and such dreadful wights
As far exceeded men in their immeasured mights[35]

Medieval chroniclers agree with Bede that Britain was formerly called Albion: Higden ascribes the name to the whiteness of its southern cliffs. Those who wrote about Brutus agree that when he arrived in England it was already inhabited by giants. Most of them do not attempt to account for the presence of giants in Britain, but some recount the Fable of Albina, which is given here in different versions, starting with a précis of that of John Strecche.

Here begins the story of how, and out of whom, this island was inhabited before the advent of Brutus, first King of Britain: it must be made clear that this is a fable, traditionally recited at countless feasts in England. Before Brutus, the island was called Albion and inhabited by giants. How do people say this came about?

There was in Greece a noble and powerful king who had thirty daughters. When they came of age, he held a great festival and invited enough princes and lords to marry all his daughters. Each one went back to her new country with her husband. Then the eldest sister wrote to them and said 'Sisters, you are most noble ladies descended from a great king. Your status is far above that of your husbands: why should you submit to their wills? Defy them and claim the freedom that is praised by the poets'. Their husbands were astonished by their behaviour and wrote to their father, the king, who summoned them all to him and told them to mend their ways. They were contrite, but the eldest called her sisters to her room and conspired with them to conceal knives and when they returned to their bedchambers, they slew their husbands while they were drugged. But the youngest sister, for love of her husband, could not kill him and when he asked her why she was so tearful, she revealed the treachery and slaughter that had occurred. All the sisters were tainted with this iniquity. From the bereaved relatives, the king learned how the princes had been killed. His daughters were brought before him and he solemnly pronounced sentence that they should die in the manner of their husbands. But his queen pleaded for him to show mercy to them. He then pronounced another fate and commuted the sentence to exile.

A boat was brought to the shore, without oars, or mast, or rudder, and his daughters set adrift upon the high seas. Neptune favoured them and abated his winds, but they were nearly swamped in a great whirlpool. On the point of exhaustion, they were beached on a great island, not yet inhabited. It was wild and verdant: there were fresh springs and delightful valleys and hills. When Dame Albina beheld the land, she claimed it and said it should be called Albion, after her own name. At first they had meagre sustenance and had to dig with their nails for the roots of herbs and search for fruit from the trees. They built shelters with branches and became healthy when they learnt how to make fire and cook meat. But they lacked the comfort of men and were consumed with desire for them, as the ancient writers tell us will always happen. Seeing this, demonic incubi lay with them, and from them they gave birth to giants. The giants bred and they occupied caves in the mountains, living at a time many years before the Trojan War. When the noble leader Brutus came to this island with his people, he landed at Totnes in Devon. He killed the giants and destroyed them, as Geoffrey of Monmouth tells us at the end of his first book. But the story of the cruel queens, and how they slew their husbands, warns us that there is no malice like the malice of women. My advice is confirmed by the philosophers Marcus Aurelius and Theophrastus. Satan uses women to tempt men and you must resist their vain beauty.

Here ends the brief account of how Britain, the great island, was inhabited by women before the advent of Brutus.

There is no name for the king, only thirty daughters, and Albina is not named until well into the story. No other versions give the diatribe against the temptations of women, which extends to more than half a page, ending 'woman, torch-bearer for the devil'- *femina phax Sathani* (Fig.10b). This seems outrageous now, but was a common medieval attitude and occurs in Chaucer, The Man of Law's Tale - which also makes use of the rudderless boat incident. It must reflect Strecche's position in charge of young men being trained as celibate priests. Indeed, this may well account for the insertion of this far-fetched tale into an otherwise scholarly work. He needed to convince his novices that they had just cause for their vow of celibacy and cited the classical philosophers to support him. Marcus Aurelius married Faustina, notorious for her profligacy and Theophrastus had an exaggerated reputation in medieval times as a misogynist, as Chaucer portrayed him.

The second Latin version is by an unknown author of a manuscript of 1366 surviving at Trinity College, Dublin, the *Eulogium Historiarum*[20], and it is given in full as Primary Source Four at the end of this book. As in Strecche, there are thirty daughters of an unnamed king. The rhetoric of Albina, who is named early on, and that of her father, is omitted and we are taken very rapidly through the first part of the story to a touching description of the dilemma of the youngest sister and great detail about making fire and the astonishing consequences of eating cooked meat! The vocabulary differs from that of Strecche and it is unlikely that it was a source for him.

The most detailed and entertaining account is that in French by Jean de Wavrin, 1394 - 1474 [19]. The histories of England and France were so intermingled that it is not surprising that some of the best chronicles were in French and, after all, French was only abandoned as the language of Law in the time of Edward III. This summary shows many details not mentioned in the other versions:

Diodicias, king of Syria, sent ambassadors to Albana, king of Cyrenia, to ask for the hand of his daughter in marriage. He had by her fourteen daughters of whom Albina was the eldest and, by three other wives, nineteen more. He invited the kings and princes under his authority to a marriage feast in Tarsus, where the daughters were all married and then betook themselves to their new countries. Albina grieved at leaving her father's court, refused to show obedience to her husband and sent secret messages to incite her sisters to acts of disobedience to their husbands. After trying every kindness, Albina's husband wrote to Diodicias informing him of his wife's ill conduct. The king ordered them all to come before him to Tyre, where he rebuked them severely. The sisters were overcome with shame and fear and implored their father's forgiveness. But when they had retired to their quarters, Albina addressed them and persuaded them to have more pride in their royal blood: *Mes seurs, bien scavez comment le roy nostre pere nous a cruellement reprinses et sy nous veult constraindre de obeir a nos maris, mais ce ne feray durant ma vie, et la cause sy est pourceque nous sommes de plus noble sang issues que ils ne sont.* She then disclosed her plan for revenge by taking daggers and cutting their throats: *Chascune de nous pourveance dun fort coutel bien trenchant adfin que une nuyt quant noz maris seront endormis nous les coppons a tous les gorges.* They pretended to be contrite and accompanied their husbands on a journey to Damascus, of which city Sardacia, the husband of Albina was king. Half-way there, Albina feigned fatigue and begged to be allowed to rest. She then sent a trusty messenger to her apothecary to prepare a sleeping potion from herbs and spices: *Adonc Albine aiant lottroy de son mary appella ung sien feable serviteur auquel elle commanda que il sen alast a Damas devers un sien apoticaire auquel elle avoit grant confidence, et lui escripvi que il feist beuvrages mestionnez de plusiers herbes et de diverses espices confite de sucre et de sinamonne, lequel beuvrage estoit tant dilicieux a boire que on ne sen pooit sauler mais tantost aprez que on lavait beu on ne desiroit que dormir.*

When they arrived in Damascus they went to the palace. Having dined, they enjoyed amusements until the evening when supper was served and the delicious potion added to the husbands' food. The princes went to their bedrooms, where Albina cut the throat of her husband while he slept and her sisters did likewise. But the youngest sister, for love of her husband, could not do the deed and related to him the whole plot: *Albine garnie dun coutel bien trenchant vint au roy Sardacia son mari sy li coppa la gorge. Et pareillement firent toutes ses aultres seurs excepte la plus josne delles qui le mieulz amoit son mari, par une grant compunction de pite qui la surmonta.* The alarm was raised and the citizens rushed to the palace and seized the sisters to protect them from the fury of the murdered princes' attendants. King Diodicias was informed and sentenced the sisters to death by burning. A council was called and the sentence was commuted to perpetual exile.

They were put in an open boat without mast or sail and left to drift on the high seas with six months' supply of food: *Et dame Albine avec toutes les aultres seurs furent condempnees estre mises en un batel sur mer sans mast et sans voille, garnie de vivres pour un demi an entier.* They were wafted through the straits of Morocco and were in great danger of perishing by storm or the attacks of sea monsters. They finally set foot on a deserted island, which Albina called Albion, after her name. They found means to make fire and caught wild beasts and birds for sustenance. But they desired the company of men, and the Devil seized his chance to make them pregnant and bear children who grew into terrible giants: *Le desir de concupiscence charnelle tant durement les surmonta que trop plus desireirent plaisir charnel que nulle aultre chose qui fust au monde. Quant le Diable qui est malicieux et soubtil sceut et perchupt le desir delles il vent en Albion sy prinst corpd dair et recueilli natures dhommes espanchies sy habita en icelles malvaises et parverses femmes de quoy elles conchuprent et a juste terme enfanterent geans grans et horribles.*

The English version of Albina in Primary Sources has been taken from Castleton's Chronicle (Primary Source 5). This is a long verse history of England edited by Professor C.D.Eckhardt[11] from the only known manuscript of about 1327 in the University library of Göttingen. 'Thomas Castleton' appears at the top of the first page but this is more likely to be the name of an owner of the manuscript than that of the author. There is no reference to the youngest daughter relenting, nor to the use of a sleeping potion. Though not of the highest quality, the verse is easy to read and remember and may well only have been written down after many years of recital at entertainments where Latin or French might not have been understood.

This fable embodies elements of Greek legend[17]. Acrisius, king of Argos, cast Danae and her son Perseus into the sea in a chest which floated to the isle of Seriphus. Aegyptus, king of Egypt, had fifty sons and forced his brother Danaüs to marry his fifty daughters, the Danaides, to them. Danaüs gave each daughter a dagger with which to kill their husbands on the bridal night, but the youngest, Hypermnestra, relented and spared her husband Lynceus. The other sisters were punished in Hades by being compelled everlastingly to fill sieves with water.

Chapter Six. Priory Books

Not a plenteous cork crop, scarcely dare we hope oak galls,
I doubt [7]

Kenilworth Priory is likely to have had its book cupboard, armarium, in the thickness of the south Transept wall, opening on to the cloister. A passageway, or slype, to the infirmary, lay between the south Transept and the Chapter House, leaving no space for a book room, as found in many other abbeys. Service books would be kept in the Church itself. At the Dissolution, Kenilworth's manuscripts were dispersed and destroyed. Apart from Strecche's two works, the only ones to survive are a Mathematical treatise in the Bodleian, Oxford, a missal in Chichester Cathedral, a history of the Francs in Berlin and some official documents.

The *Observances of Barnwell*[8], an Augustinian House in Cambridge, record many of the details of keeping the library. They stipulate that the cupboard in which the books are kept ought to be lined with wood that the damp of the walls may not moisten or stain the books - *armarium in quo libri reponuntur intrinsecus ligno vestitum esse debet ne humor parietum libros humectet vel inficiat* - and be divided by shelving on which books may be ranged so as to be separate from each other to prevent damage, or delay to those who want them. The books were laid horizontally and we can experience the same problems if we have a pile of telephone directories on a table.

The librarian was the Precentor, also responsible for music in the priory church and the conduct of services. He catalogued the volumes and kept a tally of those lent out. Keeping track of these valuable works was not easy. We know that the 13th century treatise on mathemathics and astronomy belonged to Kenilworth because of an inscription on the last page. We still have the catalogues for Titchfield Abbey and some other monasteries.

Copies of books lent by other Houses might be made in the Cloister carrels and the Precentor would provide parchment, pen and ink. If a canon wrote his own manuscript and showed pride in it, he was to be punished by a course of bread and water. This may explain Strecche's reluctance to acknowledge his authorship. Writers were not to absent themselves from services, unless special leave had been obtained from the prior, which was recited before the convent in the Chapter House. Hence Strecche's acrostic 'Prior, you have desired this work from me'.

Many books were donated by benefactors. This may account for over 150 medical books in Titchfield Abbey catalogue[45], few of which were written after the mid-13th century. This small abbey had more than one thousand works, collected in 224 volumes, yet its historical books were limited to only seven: a poem on the Fall of Troy (not the author copied by Strecche), the Prophecies of Merlin by Geoffrey of Monmouth, three books about Alexander the Great, one about Guy of Warwick (in French), and the Fable of Albina listed as *De origine gigancium*. This was possibly the version printed as a Primary Source 4 at the end of this book. The library of Lincoln Cathedral Chapter[42] has one hundred pre-reformation manuscripts, three medical, a herbal, and only six historical: four of these are Bede's *History of the English Church and People*, Geoffrey of Monmouth's *History of the Kings of Britain*, Guido de Colonne's *History of Troy*, and Higden's *Polychronicon*. Strecche refers to all these in his work. If Kenilworth were similarly deficient in historical books, it is not surprising that he relied so much on Higden to prompt his memory of anything he learnt elsewhere. Oxford University operated the *pecia* system[6], where a text exemplar was divided into its constituent quires, which were lent to students for reading or copying. This was Strecche's chance to acquire his own copy of a chronicle.

His manuscript is on vellum, calf-skin prepared by soaking in lime for nine days[12]. The underlying flesh was then scraped off one side, and the hair, epidermis and part of the dermis was

Fig.7a. The entrance to the Library at Valle Crucis Abbey near Llangollen. The room is scarcely more than a book cupboard built in the thickness of the west wall of the Chapter House, yet its importance is shown by the decorated stone screen.

Fig.7b. Marginal drawings in Strecche's manuscript about Burnellus the ass, and Bernardus his master.

scraped off the other side, using a fleshing knife. The skin was rubbed smooth with chalk and pumice and then stretched across a frame. A few of the pages of his manuscript have the dermis insufficiently scraped and show the hair follicles as stippling of part of the page. On one folio he has to write around the scar of a skin wound or the exit hole of a warble fly. Four sheets of skin were folded once to give a quire of eight leaves or folios: since each folio has two surfaces, this provides sixteen pages. The pages were numbered long after the Dissolution, and rather confusingly, as folio recto and folio verso. Before folding the four skins, the scribes gave them a quire letter and sheet number[26]: i.e. *ai, aii, aiii, aiiii.* These signatures are very instructive: they indicate missing folios and suggest how the book might have been put together. To keep track of the unbound pages, at the end of some quires, Strecche wrote two catch words in a box, which duplicated the first two words of the next quire (e.g. '*e8*' fo.269v and *fi* fo.270). Blank spaces were wasteful of expensive vellum and he usually filled them with a guide to the previous - *explicit* - or following - *incipit* - contents.

Strecche followed standard practice in ruling the margins of the pages, using plummet, a bar of lead. For his prologue, he wrote carefully on ruled horizontal lines: for the rest of the History, he wrote freehand within the frame, so the number of lines per page varies from 35 to 42. This is characteristic of quickly written student textbooks[9]. However, he did take trouble to start each chapter with a two to four line capital initial in red or blue, extended into marginal calligraphic decoration above and below. The colours must have been imported. Red came from dried females of the *Kermes* coccid bug, or from the Mediterranean turn-sole plant, *Chrozophora tinctoria,* whose juice from the stems or roots changes colour like litmus. Blue came from azurite, a hydrated copper carbonate, or just possibly luxurious lapis lazuli, since Kenilworth was a prosperous House. Lapis lazuli, a complex aluminium silicate with sulphur imparting the blue, could be obtained only from Kokcha in Afghanistan. These colours were bound with clarea, cleared egg white. A 15th century recipe for black ink required powdered oak galls, copperas (iron sulphate) and gum arabic, to be strained through canvas. The galls were hard brown marble galls, not the fleshy pink and green true oak apples. They must have been imported since the gall wasp that produces them cannot complete its life cycle without Turkey oaks, not introduced into England until 1735. Iron sulphate reacts with their tannin to produce pale iron II tannate, which oxidises on the page to intense black iron III tannate. Over the centuries, this has faded to dark brown. Carbon ink was also used, and does not fade. Ink was held in an ox-horn on the side of the writing desk. The gum content was crucial: too little and the ink would sink in, too much and it would flake off. The ink had to be left to dry and not be blotted and this gave the scribe a chance to rest after each recto before turning the folio to write its verso. A blunt knife was needed to smooth the parchment surface, and a sharp knife to cut the goose feather quill or erase dried mistakes: bread crumbs were used to erase wet mistakes. Scribes often protested that their work was arduous: 'he who cannot write thinks it is not a labour - three fingers write but the whole body aches'[26]. They were urged to fear Titivillus, the copyists' demon, seeking out the slightest mistake and carrying on his back a sack of forgotten syllables which would be taken into account at the Last Judgement.

His text is written in Anglicana Formata Hybrida script, popular in the 14th and 15th centuries for lower and middle grade books, characterised by rounded loops and a closed *s*. This script permitted rapid copying and its introduction has been associated with the growth of the libraries of monasteries in the late 14th century[31]. It is heavily abbreviated and somewhat confusing to the modern eye. *n* or *m* are often denoted by a dash somewhere over a syllable, *per* by a stroke across the descender of *p*, and *pro* by a circumflex over the *p*. Strecche favoured a diphthong *oe* for *e*: his *f* is easily mistaken for an *s*, although he sometimes helps by writing by writing *f* as *ff*. Chapters are numbered using Arabic numerals in the margin, but all dates in the text are in Roman numerals. Chapter headings are written as a rubric: red ink flowed better than any other colour (unfortunately it does not photograph well!). They were added after the text was written and Strecche often left inadequate room for them.

When and where did he write? He finishes the book with the death of King Henry V, 1422. Recording the death of Owen Glendower in Chapter 10 of Book Five Henry IV, Strecche comments that the Welsh lived peacefully during the reign of Henry V: this makes it likely that at least everything that followed was written after 1422. He was Prior of Brooke until 1425, so may well have been writing much of the history at Brooke, rather than at Kenilworth.

The Appendix, and Fig.8 with its description, will help when reading the following paragraph. Figs.8,9,10 could be copied to A4 or A3 size to be made more legible.

The first part of his History to be written may have been the *History of England in Five Books*. This runs from quire *a1* to *g3* (folios 233 to 279). He then wanted to extend his history back in time, so he asked his pupil John Aston (possibly Arton) to start a new series of quires copying out the *History of Troy*, *a1* to *r4* and the *History of the Kings of Britain*, running from *r5* to *s8* and a second *a1* to *k8*. (Folios *5* to *8* were not marked, but are the folded portions of *1* to *4*). John Aston copies carefully in a squarer hand which is easier to read than his busy master's: he ruled horizontal lines - the pricking can be seen on some pages - and wrote with carbon ink which has remained black. Strecche read through his student's work and marked it with 'correct', *cor*, at each quire end. The verso of *r4* is folio 136v, which leaves a large space filled by Strecche with explanations of what he has included: this folio appears at the end of this Chapter. The verso of *'k8'* leaves a very small space and Strecche is hard put to it to write his *explicit* - here ends the *History of the Kings of Britain*, and *incipit* - here begins my *History of England*. But the History doesn't begin for another eight pages: he decides to insert an unlettered two sheet quire to explain why Brutus found giants in England, so he writes the Fable of Albina, finishing with a dire warning about women for his celibate novices. Since there is no room to change *k8*, he adds a line to the already rather chaotic rubrics on fo.136v. He is keen to start Book IV, England after the Norman Conquest with accounts of Kenilworth Priory, on a new page, so at the end of Book III he uses the remaining third of fo.246v to explain the acrostic of his name derived from the chapter initials of Books I to III: *Johannes Strecche canonicus.* Perhaps he wrote these books while a student taking Holy Orders at St Frideswide's Augustinian Priory (College) at Oxford, making a précis of Higden, and amusing his fellow students by making the acrostic. Later, his Prior, Thomas Kidderminster, requested him to expand the work into a full textbook of English history, so he became less reticent about his authorship and finally designed an ornamental frontispiece, with his initials writ large in blue and red, below which is an acrostic giving his name and acting as both a brief preface and a dedication. Curiously, he did not give a title and the book mistakenly became known as a history of Troy.

Strecche's piety is shown even in Book Five. After recording the burial of Thomas, Duke of Clarence, Henry V's brother, Chapter 26, he writes a short sermon:

> Almighty God, how false and fragile are the glories of this world, whose prosperity is transitory. The mighty fall as quickly as a potter's vase may shatter. This the poet reveals in verse....

There follow two lines from the 12th century Nigel of Canterbury's *Speculum Stultorum.* Since Strecche had copied out this poem himself in his Miscellany, presumably he deliberately gave no reference, leaving his students to hunt it out for themselves.

That part of Book Five which refers to Henry V has been studied by Frank Taylor[41]. He regards Strecche's historical accounts of the wars in France as careless and showing a strong prejudice in favour of the English, hardly surprising. However, the great fondness of King Henry V for Kenilworth, and the undoubted connections between the Priory and the Castle, would have given Strecche unrivalled opportunities to pick up gossip from the Castle, its royal servants and even its prisoners. Taylor identifies Strecche's more reliable accounts particularly the Story of the Tennis-balls. This is told in Shakespeare's *King Henry V*, Act 1, scene ii:

> *French Ambassador:* The Prince our master says that you savour too much of your youth: you cannot revel into

dukedoms in France. He therefore sends you, meeter for your spirit, this tun of treasure and desires you let the dukedoms that you claim hear no more of you.

King Henry: What treasure, Uncle?

Exeter: Tennis-balls, my liege.

King Henry: We are glad the Dauphin is so pleasant with us. When we have matched our rackets to these balls, we will in France, by God's grace, play a set shall strike his father's crown into the hazard. ... Tell the pleasant prince this mock of his hath turned his balls to gun-stones and his soul shall stand sore charged for the wasteful vengeance that shall fly with them.

Strecche's earlier version is closer to reality and I am very grateful to Brian Jackson for his permission to quote from his article[29], with translations, in *Kenilworth History, 2000-2001*:

Strecche gives some account of the failure of the negotiations with the French over Henry's proposed marriage, *inter Henricum regem Angelorum et nobilem dominam Katerinam regis francorum filiam*. He is much more specific about what followed: 'These French, blinded by their own arrogance, and careless of the dreadful consequences, vomited forth words of venom - *verbis fellis eructantes* - to the English envoys. The French told the departing English delegation that because Henry was young, they would send him tennis balls to play with, and some soft pillows to sleep on to help him grow to manly strength'.

'When these insults were reported to the King, he was greatly moved: 'With words brief, well-chosen and graceful in form, this is what he said: If God wills, and I have life and health, within a few short months, I shall play such games with my cannon balls within their streets that the French will curse their mockery and pay for their wit with tears and lamentations.'

After the Dissolution the first manuscript passed through the hands of Thomas Morrow, a 16th Century antiquary, and was

44

sold from the library of Bertram, 4th Earl of Ashburnam in 1899 to the British Museum. The Museum published a description in 1901 (now available on the British Library website), headed 'A Collection of Romance and English History', although it is now apparent that it is a more coherent book than this description would imply. The description was possibly written by C.L.Kingsford, who referred to it in a series of published lectures given in Oxford and tantalisingly said that the chronicle should be included in full in his book but there was not room. The greater part of Book Five, for the reign of Henry V, was transcribed in Latin by Frank Taylor, later Keeper of Medieval Manuscripts for the John Ryland Library, with many useful footnotes. Later authors have referred to Kingsford's and Taylor's work but it has not been possible to trace any other transcription or translation. A microfilm of the Chronicle manuscript from fo.229 is held by Warwickshire County Record Office (MI393). Further transcription and translation of the History is in progress and should reveal fascinating details of construction of the Priory buildings and the Priors who initiated them.

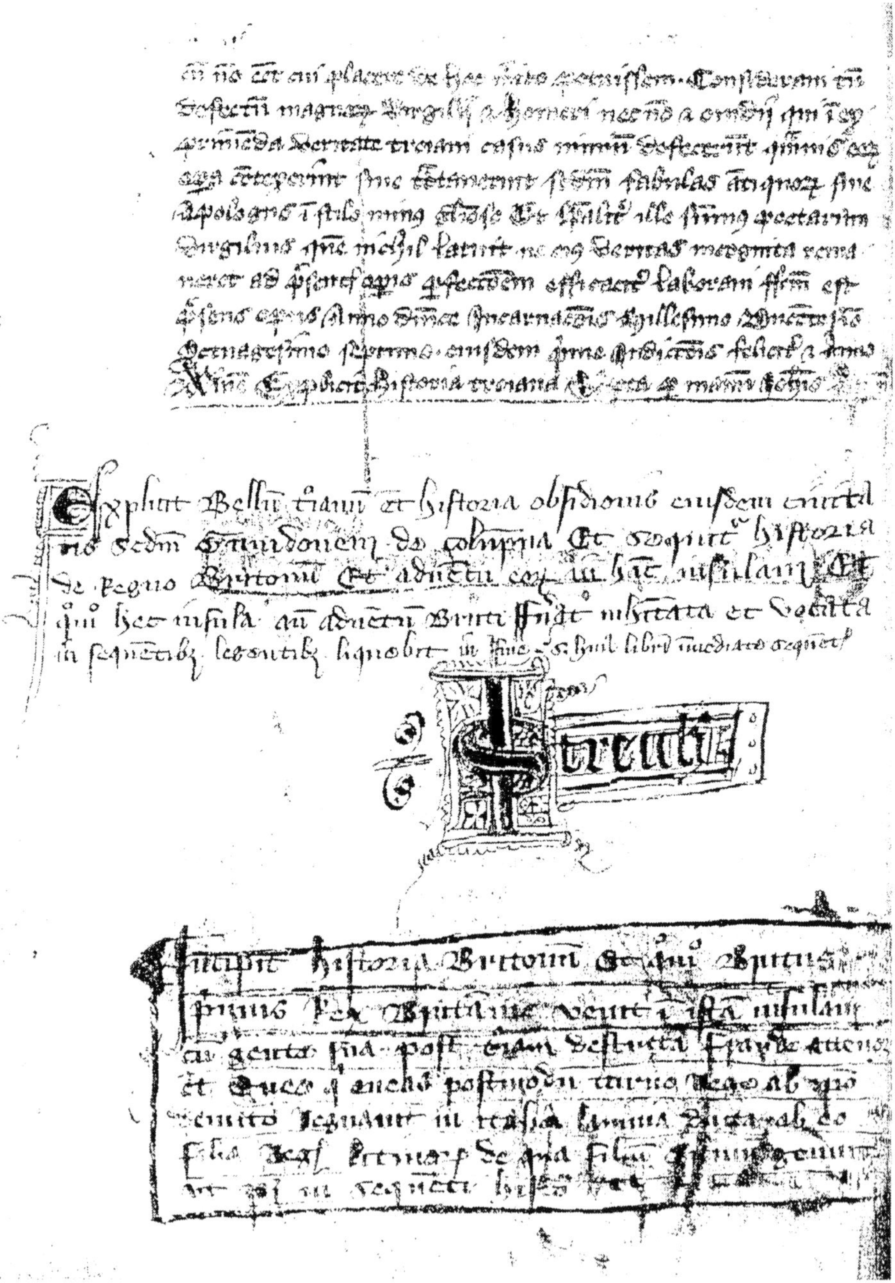

Fig.8. Fo.136v End of *History of Troy* and beginning of *History of Britain*, with 'signature' of Strecche. British Library Additional Manuscript 35295 fo.136v. See description opposite.

Description of fo.136v, Add.MS 35295.

End of Epilogue by Guido delle Colonne to his Historia Trojana.

Lines 7-9:
I have laboured for the perfection of these works. Written in the year of the Incarnation of Our Lord 1287.
Line 10:
Amen. Here ends the History of Troy, copied by the hand of John Arton.

Explicit by John Strecche:

Lines 11-15:
Here ends the story of Troy and the siege of that same city, told by Guido delle Colonne. There follows the story of the kingdom of Britain and the coming of some of the Trojans. And how this island, before the coming of Brutus, was inhabited, yet forbidden. All will be revealed in a careful reading of the following books.

Line 16: J.Strecche, 'signature'

Incipit by John Strecche:

Lines 17-19:
Here begins the story of Britain and how Brutus, its first king, came to the island with his people after Troy had been weakened by trickery and destroyed.

Strecche finds there is still space to be filled on the precious vellum, so he goes back to the ancestry of Brutus.

Lines 20-23:
After the siege of Troy, Aeneas deposed King Turnus and reigned in Italy with Lavinia: his descendants are described in the following history

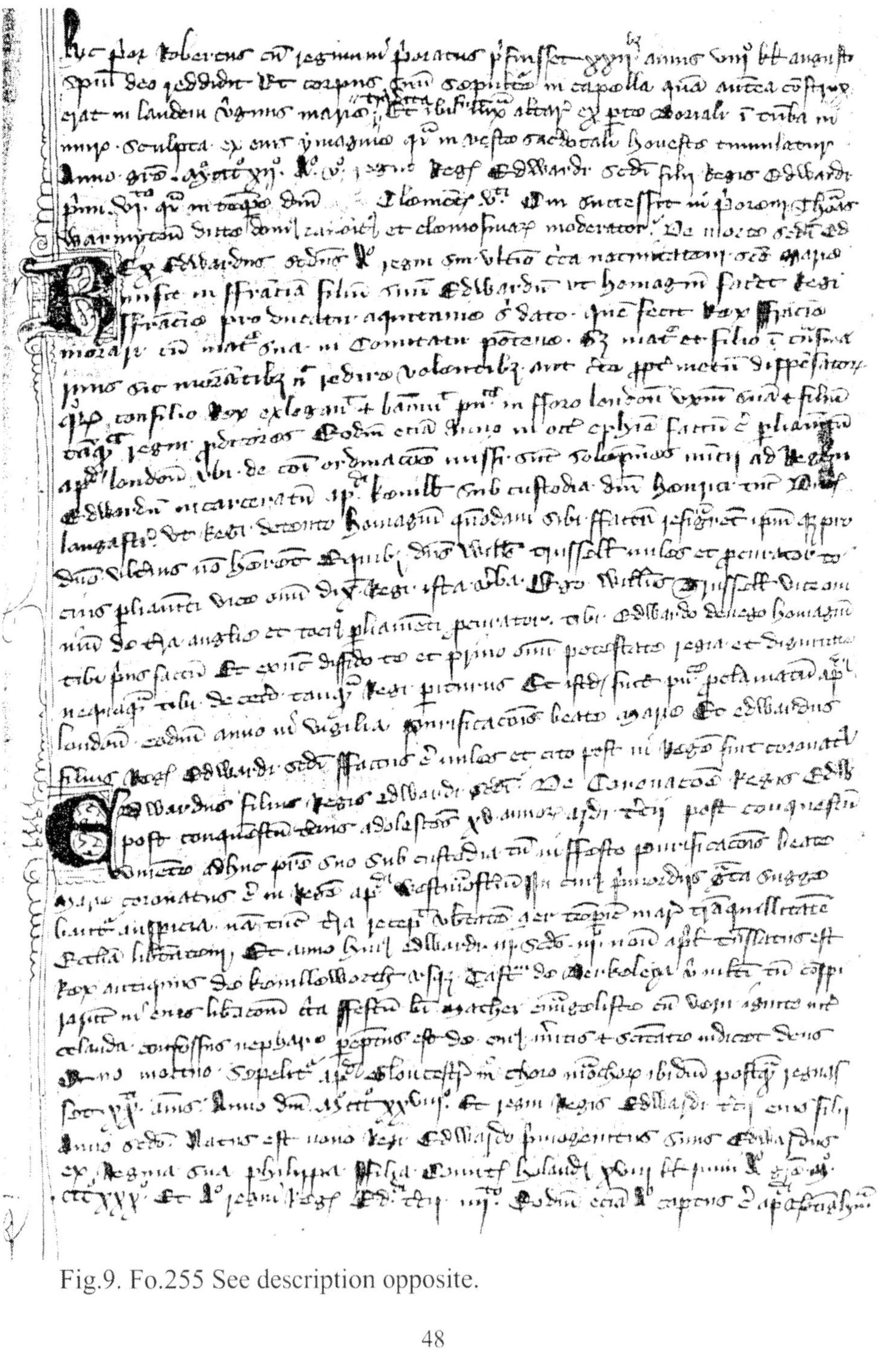

Fig.9. Fo.255 See description opposite.

End of Chapter 36: rubric 'Robert Salle Prior'

Lines 1-6: *Prior Robert of Kenilworth gave his spirit to God and his body to be buried in the Chapel in praise of the Virgin Mary, which he had built, with an effigy in priestly vestments*[25], *1312, 5th year of the reign of Edward II, son of Edward I, sixth year of the pontificate of Clement V.*

Lines 6-7: *His successor was Thomas Warmington.*

Chapter 37: rubric 'Death of Edward II' (in fact his deposition, his death following in Chapter 38).

Lines 8-14: Higden p.318, with the omission of one sentence

The King sends his son to do homage in France. Queen and son refuse to return through fear of the Despensers and are denounced as traitors.

Lines 14-24: Higden p.322. The execution of the Despensers and return of the Queen and her son, p.320, has surprisingly been omitted, but the renouncement by Trussell is quoted in full.

The King is imprisoned at Kenilworth: Parliament in London rejects the King and Sir William Trussell renounces his duty of homage.

Chapter 38: rubric 'Coronation of Edward III after the Conquest'.

Lines 25-33: Higden p.324.

Edward, the son of Edward, the third after the conquest, a youth of fifteen, is crowned. The beginning of his reign is auspicious. The former King is taken from Kenilworth to Berkeley and barbarously murdered (Strecche changes Higden's *ignominiose* to *nephare*, line 33) *wherefore many say he died a martyr.*

Lines 33-34: Strecche's own.

Burial of the former King in the monk's choir of Gloucester Abbey.

Lines 35-38: Higden p.326, but Strecche names his mother as Queen Philippa and does not call him Edward IV.

Birth of the first son of Edward III. Capture at (N)ottingham.... (of Roger Mortimer).

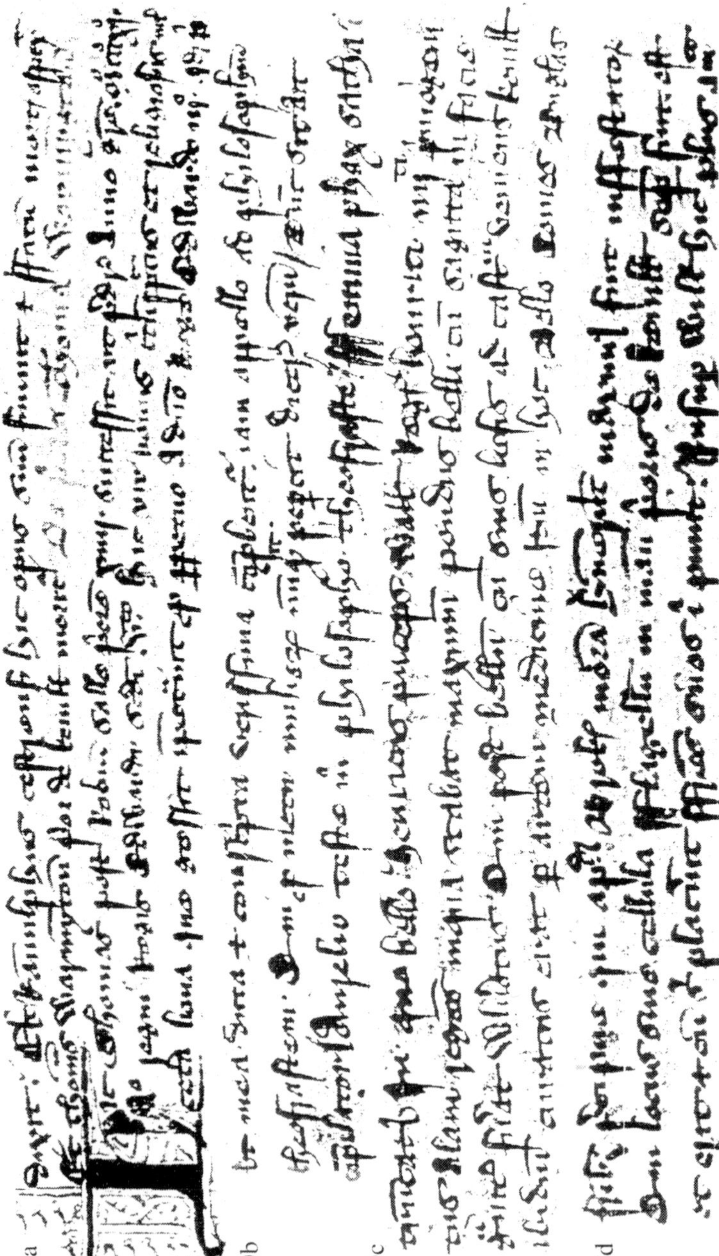

Fig.10. Facsimile extracts from four folios.
See References: List of Folio numbers cited in text.

10a. fo.255v   10b. fo.232   10c. fo.263v   10d. fo.253v

Chapter Seven. The Miscellany

At first glance, the Miscellany is a collection of dull medieval texts. On further examination, it has much to tell us about Strecche and his times. There are ten texts in the collection, mostly in his own hand.

The first four manuscripts are about Augustinian business, but include verses by Strecche himself against the Austin friars making claims to be true Augustinians. The Friars were a threat to the established canons and monks because of their greater popularity: they were freer to move amongst the people, preaching to them and educating them and did not isolate themselves in large buildings.

In the fifth manuscript, Strecche again employs verse, this time as a lesson on thirty patterns, or colours, of rhyming verse. Whereas the Cistercians frowned upon poetry, the Augustinians encouraged it, as a form of rhetoric to teach, delight, move and persuade. The term 'colours' was used for some of the stylistic ornaments of rhetoric and Strecche may have been borrowing this term for his list of patterns of rhyming. His first colour was Leonine hexameters, where the final syllable of six metrical feet rhymes with the third. The last practitioner of this in English verse (hopefully) was Lord Tennyson in his poem of Hesper and Rosalind:

Low-flying breezes are roaming

the broad valley dimmed in the gloaming

Following this, Strecche copies out couplets from the Latin moralist Cato. He lived in the 2nd or 3rd century A.D. and 'The Cato' was standard material for teaching Latin in the Middle

Ages. The first three couplets copied by Strecche (transcription and translation by Jim Marchand, University of Pennsylvania) are:

If God is a spirit as the songs tell us
He is to be worshipped above all with a pure mind
Si Deus est animus nobis ut carmina dicunt
Hic tibi praecipue sit pura mente colendus
Always keep alert nor be given to sleep
For continuous idleness offers food for vice
Plus vigila semper nec somno deditus esto
Nam diuturna quies vitiis alimenta ministrat
I think the first virtue is to be keeping your tongue
He is close to God who knows how to keep quiet properly
Virtutem primam esse puto compescere linguam
Proximus ille deo est qui scit ratione tacere

Strecche would recognise that the novices deserved some lighter, even humorous, reading. So he copies out sixty of Aesop's Fables. At the end he feels somewhat regretful about this levity and finishes with the penitent prayer

Have mercy on Thy servant John Strecche, enfolding him in Thy mantle
Involvens pannis puerum miserere Iohannis Strecche

His final manuscript in the Miscellany, probably copied out by himself judging by the ornamentation, is *The Mirror of Fools* by Nigel Wireker. This is the most interesting of the contents, not least because we have evidence that the young canons actually read it! Marginal sketches of a leech with a face, various asses, a bishop's mitre, and a hare, all show that it has been enjoyed by its readers. Drawing in library books is not to be encouraged, but antiquity lends excuse for these windows into the medieval mind. The book was written by a monk of Christ Church Canterbury, not later than 1180. It was a poem of nearly 4000 lines and one of the most popular medieval satires. Even the fox in Chaucer's Nun's Priest's Tale had read about Burnel the Ass.

It tells of the ass Burnellus who goes in search of a longer tail. He consults Galen, who sends him to Salerno with a prescription. On the way back he is robbed of the glass bottles and half his short tail. Afraid to return home, he attends the University of Paris for seven years but on leaving, he even forgets the name of the place. He then hopes to found a new religious Order, taking all the easiest rules of the existing Orders. But Bernard his master catches up with him and takes him home to Cremona, saying 'You may send an ass to Paris, but if he's an ass here, he won't be a horse there'.

Burnellus represents the discontented, ambitious monk. Nigel himself attended the English School at the University of Paris, where he found English students praised for their generosity and other virtues, but too much addicted to wassail cup.

It is not likely that these texts were bound together when Strecche was using them. The *Mirror for Fools* would most likely be lent out on its own to students and other teachers, which would account for the note of names of some borrowers on the last page of this text. A precentor librarian able to buy Caxton's modern printed versions could well have tidied the book cupboard after Strecche had left, using the even older redundant manuscripts which have provided the binding for this volume.

A List of Contents of the Miscellany ends this Chapter.

Contents of British Library Additional Manuscript 38665

1. Verses against the Austin Friars for representing Augustine in opposition to the claims of the Austin Canons. Fo.5.

2. A counterblast against the work of an Austin Friar claiming priority for his Order. Fos.6-14. Not in the hand of Strecche.

3. List of names of Augustinian Priors. Fos.15-18. Not in the hand of Strecche.

4. Chronicle of some Chapters of Augustinians 1325-1350. Fos.19-32. Not in the hand of Strecche.

5. Treatise on thirty different colours of rhyming verse. Fos.33-35.

6. *Liber Catonis*, the Book of Cato. Moral distichs in hexameter verse attributed to Dionysius Cato. Fos.35v-40.

7. *Esopus in fabulis*, Aesop's Fables. Fos.41-55.

8. *Ymago mundi*, View of the World by Honorius Augustodunensis. Fos.57-85. Hand of 12th-13th century. A treatise on astronomy and meteorology, relating them to heaven and earth and the soul, by a prolific writer of the 12th century.

9. *Speculum stultorum*, The Mirror for Fools by Nigel Wireker. Fos.85-168.

10. Various Sermons. Fos.169-186. Hand of 12th-13th century.

Chapter 8. Prior of Brooke

Kenilworth Priory, an Abbey from 1447, had a dependent cell at Brooke, near Oakham in Rutland founded 1135-54 [38]. Of the very little we know about John Strecche, it is certain that he was Prior of Brooke from 1407 to 1425 [40]. He makes only one significant comment about Brooke Priory: this Chapter is an attempt to add the flesh of speculation to the scant bones of fact and construct a picture of the life he may have led there.

While at Brooke, he was isolated with only two to four canons, some of whom might have been sent there as punishment for their wrong-doings at Kenilworth. He would need to treat them with firmness, yet humanity. He would also have to uphold the right of distant Kenilworth to possess this small Priory against local bishops, abbeys and landowners who saw it as a tempting prize of land and income.

All this must have been in his mind when he wrote (Fig.10d), with surprising criticism, about Prior William de Evesham, tenth Prior of Kenilworth, 1276 - 1280:

> 'This Prior William was haughty and unpleasant to his Brethren and severe in his regime. Any troublesome Brother was sent without delay to Brooke, which place of punishment was, is, and always shall be, in the hands of the Priors of Kenilworth - *qui locus sive cellula flagellum in manum prioris de Kenill semper fuit est et erit* - and while there Brethren atone for their wrong-doing.'

Here again is Strecche writing his chronicle for the instruction of novices at Kenilworth. This passage not only warns them about the possibility of punishment but also instructs them in the importance of Brooke being kept in the possession of Kenilworth. In fact it slipped out of the hands of the Abbot of Kenilworth two years before the Dissolution.

Nevertheless, he must have found this appointment rewarding, for he stayed eighteen years, more than twice the average length of service for Priors of Brooke, many of whom lasted only for two or three years. Perhaps it gave him the chance to concentrate on the task of writing his chronicle, equipped with the history notes he must have made as a student, a supply of vellum sheets, quills and ink.

Chaucer, in his jocular way, wrote only twenty years earlier about the temptations open to the Prior of a small monastic cell when he describes the monk in *The Canterbury Tales*. Brian Jackson has kindly contributed the following version for this book:

> There was a monk, at the top of his profession, who spent his time outside the monastery riding round the estates and enjoying the hunt. ... He had many a handsome mount in his stables and the bells on his bridle called as clear and loud as the chapel bell at the cell where he was in charge. ... He kept greyhounds swift as birds in flight and on no account would he give up his tracking and hunting the hare. He did not agree in the slightest that hunters are unholy men, or that a monk outside his cloister is a fish out of water. ... Why should he drive himself mad with study, poring over books in a cloister? Or toil with his hands, as St Augustine wished? Augustine can keep the hard work all to himself! ... His sleeves were trimmed at the wrist with costly fur and to fasten his hood under his chin, he had a pin made of gold. A roasted fat swan was his favourite dish.

Chaucer's monk is a satirical fictional portrait and there is of course no reason to suppose that John Strecche was anything other than conscientious and pious, but I hope he had some relaxation and enjoyment in the pleasant shire of Rutland.

Travelling to and from the two Houses must have been an interesting and somewhat perilous experience. Brooke is sixty

Fig.11a. 13th century tower
(with later battlements) of
St Peter's Church Brooke,
near Oakham, Rutland.

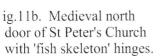

ig.11b. Medieval north
door of St Peter's Church
with 'fish skeleton' hinges.

miles from Kenilworth and would be a considerable journey for a moderate horseman, possibly with an interlude at the great Augustinian Abbey of Leicester. I am indebted to Sue Hutchins of Castle Barn, Kenilworth, for the following account of the logistics of the journey:

> A journey of sixty miles would have taken about two and a half to three days. This is assuming the horse travelled at about four miles per hour. Rest stops and frequent water stops would be necessary at rivers and streams. The horse would graze at these points. Presumably the canon would take refreshment and fodder should have been provided for the horse or pony.

> Provided the horse was rested overnight in a stable, it would be capable of this type of journey. The pony type would probably have been the predecessor of the Welsh cob, stocky and surefooted.

A party from a religious house could be carrying treasure and money and would need servants with weapons to ward off robbers.

Only an elevated field marks the site of the Priory today, but a mile away lies the church of St Peter, Brooke. He must have visited this church frequently, worshipped there, and discussed the business of the church and manor, which had been granted to Kenilworth Priory. A statuette in Bushmead Priory, Bedfordshire, of a canon going outside his monastery, shows a girdle from which hangs a bookcase on his left, a purse or pen case on his right, while he holds a missal in his left hand and a staff in his right hand.

The church was rebuilt in Elizabethan times, but many features he must have known still exist there. As a historian, he would appreciate the 13th century tower, Norman font and internal arcade, and no doubt been amused by the fish-skeleton hinges on the north door. His Priory may also have kept and venerated a saint's relic in the elaborate Limoges enamel reliquary now to be seen in Rutland County Museum at Oakham.

Chapter 9. Shades of Kenilworth Priory

Here in this open court, which now lies naked
to the injuries of stormy weather,
Some men lie interred loved the church so well
and gave so largely to it
They thought it should have canopied their bones
till doomsday [3]

Strecche would have been devasted by the Dissolution and destruction of his Priory, about which he wrote, more than once, that it would exist in perpetuity. However, he would be heartened by the events which have occurred at the turn of the 20th and 21st centuries to reincarnate the ruins.

By comparison with Hailes, Tintern or the great Yorkshire Abbeys, there is little to see of Kenilworth Abbey and even some long-term residents have been unaware of its existence or confuse the Abbey Church with the much smaller and later Parish Church. The Kenilworth History and Archaeology Society reopened The Barn Museum in the 1970s, and the Kenilworth Abbey Advisory Committee raised money for the restoration of the Gatehouse in 1977, and improved the Museum by adding an upper floor in 1994. Mr Jeff Watkin of Warwick District Council Leisure and Amenities Department suggested a more ambitious scheme to present the Abbey to Kenilworth people and visitors, and application was made for a grant from the Heritage Lottery Fund. This was successful, and in 1999 the Kenilworth Abbey Interpretation Scheme began, with a grant of £78 700 from the Heritage Lottery

Fund, £15 425 from Warwick District Council and £5 000 from Kenilworth Town Council[30].

The scheme was developed and managed professionally by Warwick District Council, The Drawing Room of Warwick and the University of Warwick, with much unpaid effort by local people and Societies, and has resulted in several achievements: a Research Associate was appointed to provide new academic insight for the Scheme; a major new exhibition has been mounted on the ground floor of The Barn, with associated archaeological investigations being made while making the floor and walls sound - there are striking reconstructions from the original stones of the vaulting ribs and blind arcading from the Chapter House; a series of explanatory plaques has been designed and erected, four large ones at entrances to Abbey Fields as part of a trail linked to the Town and the Castle; thirteen small bronze plaques have been fixed on walls or in the ground in different parts of the ruins; there is a website, *www.kenilworthabbey.org* ; a free explanatory leaflet on card has been published for visitors to the exhibition and tourists, enabling self-guiding round the ruins.

The Research Associate was Dr Christine Hodgetts of Warwick University and her rediscovery of the importance of Additional Manuscript 35295 is explained on one of the panels in The Barn exhibition. From the manuscript she identified the damaged effigy in the North Transept as that of Prior Robert Salle[25]. She also rekindled much interest in the manuscript and its author John Strecche - as this book attests.

Fortuitously, there was a collapse of ground in Abbey Fields in May of the Millennium Year 2000. This was excavated by Dr Stephen Hill of the University of Warwick, who identified it as an access shaft to the culvert for the Priory water supply. This had previously been known only from a Charter of Henry III [40], granting the Priory the right to take water from the grounds of Edith Lawerthin, who lived in the vicinity of the Castle, so long as she was compensated for damage when constructing it.

Fig.12. The first Communion Service held on the site of St Mary's Abbey Church since 1538, on 29th June, 2003.

Photograph by P.R.Alford.

A few objects other than stonework provide a reminder of Strecche's Priory. In St Mary's Church, Halford, there is a canon's stall with a 15th century misericord carved with a bearded man performing a tumbling trick: this is believed to have come from Kenilworth Abbey[44]. Lying near the lectern in St Nicholas' Church Kenilworth is a pig, or fodder, of lead melted down from the roofs. Someone had attempted to cheat King Henry VIII of his plunder, but being over half a tonne in weight, it was not easy to spirit away and remained buried until 1888. While the Castle has many street-names in Kenilworth to commemorate it, the Abbey has very few, but 2003 saw St Mary's Court adopted at the suggestion of this author[22].

Apart from his own manuscript, only three books have survived from the Priory Library. One is a manuscript in the Bodleian Library, Oxford, (MS.Auct.F.3.13), being a collection of mathematical and astronomical texts. The last page bears an inscription in a 15th century hand, which proclaims that it was bequeathed to the monastery at Kenilworth, in perpetuity, by John Alward, Rector of Stoke Bruerne. The present Rector tells me that John Alward was Rector there from 1420 - 1457, so it is unlikely that Strecche would have read or seen it, unless for some reason John Alward had spent some time in the Priory. The parchment is warped and shows signs of having been left out in the rain, perhaps retrieved from the flames of the lead-melting fires, or snatched from being torn apart for packing material, by one of the far-sighted antiquaries who tried to rescue these precious books. Chichester Cathedral possesses an illuminated missal made for the Prior of Kenilworth, including a prayer for the Founders, and Strecche may have seen it or possibly read from it.

The awakened interest in the Abbey led to the first Communion service since 1538 being held on the site in June 2003, attended by over 250 people. More than the recognition of his manuscript, this would surely have rejoiced the spirit of

JOHN STRECCHE, CANON OF KENILWORTH.

Appendix: Guide to Quires Q), Folios and Chapters (Ch.) of Additional Manuscript 35295, John Strecche.

1v   Calendar fragment   bcdefg repeated

2v   IS monogram and a sentence for preface and
         dedication, forming acrostic 'Ion Strecche'

3-4v   Poem   The Fall of Troy

5   Calendar fragment

Qa1. 6   IS monogram. Prologue for the following work:
         History of Troy by G. della Colonne, in 37 books

   7   *History of Troy*   (copied in the hand of J.Aston)

Qr4. 136   Conclusion to *History of Troy*

    136v   End of *History of Troy*, (J.A.). 12 line summaries in
         hand of J.Strecche: 'End of Trojan War by G de
         Colonne', IS signature, 'Beginning *History of
         Britain*, how Brutus became first King after the Fall
         of Troy'

   137   *History of Britain* by Geoffrey of Monmouth in 8
         books (copied in the hand of J.Aston)

Qs1. 141

Qa1. 149

Qk8. 228v   End of *History of Britain*, with warning to William
         of Malmesbury and Henry of Huntingdon.
         (Remainder of the whole Manuscript in the hand of
         John Strecche). 5 line summary 'End of History of
         Britain. Beginning History of England before the
         monarchy and after the expulsion of the Britons,
         until the time of Henry VI, in 5 books'. (In fact this
         begins on fo.233).

Q-1. 229 (Inserted half quire) Brief history from Brutus to 827 AD
         W,S, and E Saxons, E Angles, Bernicia, their river
         boundaries, British driven beyond Severn, record of
         Bede.

    230 Vortigern. Begin history of how this island was
         inhabited before Brutus arrived: the fable of Albina,
         origin of the name Albion.

    232 Diatribe against women. End of brief chronicle
         before Brutus (232v - lacuna, i.e.blank)

Qa1. 233 **BOOK 1** Ch.1: **I** Begin history of reign of Saxons in England: Vortigern reigned in Britain (i.e.Wales). Initial letters of Chapter headings form the acrostic Johannes Strecche canonicus.

233v Augustine sent by Gregory in 597.

234 Ch.2: **O** East Angles
234v Ch.3: **H** Northumbria, reference to Bede and others
236 Ch.4: **A** Mercia
237 Ch.5: **N** West Saxons
238 Ch.6: **N** Egbert
238v Ch.7: **E** Aethelwulf
Ch.8: **S** Aethelred

239 **BOOK 2.** Ch.1: **S** Alfred,verse 239v,Saxon monarchs
239v Ch.2: **T** Edward
240 Ch.3: **R** Athelstan
240v Ch.4: **E** Edmund, verse (Catchwords for Qb1.)
Qb1. 241 Ch.5: **C** Edred
Ch.6: **C** Edwig
Ch.7: **H** Edgar, verse 241v
242 Ch.8: **E** St Edward, King and Martyr
Ch.9: **C** Ethelred

242v **BOOK 3.** Ch.1: **A** Danish monarchs, Edm.Ironside
243v Ch.2: **N** Canute
244 Ch.3: **O** Harold Harefoot
Ch.4: **N** Hardicanute
244v Ch.5: **I** St Edward, King and Confessor
245 Ch.6: **C** Harold, son of Earl Godwin
245v Ch.7: **U** William, Duke of Normandy
246 Ch.8: **S** Battle of Hastings
246v End of Book 3, rubric summarising Books 1 - 3 and revealing acrostic from initial letters of Chapters
247 **BOOK 4.** from Norman Conquest to Henry IV, including Chapters about Priors.
247 Ch. 1: William the Bastard

64

	247v	Ch. 2:	William Rufus
	248		Ch. 3: Henry I
	248	Ch. 4:	....
	248v	Ch. 5:	Stephen and Matilda (Catchword)
Qc1?		Chapters 6 to 13 missing: Stephen, Henry II, and 3 Priors	
Qc5?	249	Ch.14:	Priory Founders, Henry II
	249	Ch.15:	Richard I
	249v	Ch.16:	John, verse
	250	Ch.17:	Prior Sylvester,1186, Walter,1203
	250	Ch.18:	Prior William,1217
	250v	Ch.19:	....
	251	Ch.20:	....
	251v	Ch.21:	Henry III, verse
	252	Ch.22:	.... verse
	252	Ch.23:	....
	252v	Ch:24:	...
	252v	Ch.25:	....
	252v	Ch.26:	....
	252v	Ch.27:	.... (Catchword)
		Chapter 28 missing	
Qd2	253	Ch.29:	Prior Nicholaus
	253	Ch.30:	Priors William,Wilfred, Robert, King Henry III
	253v	Ch.31 (numbered 32): Edward I	
	253v	Ch.32 (numbered 33): Prior1270	
	253v	Ch.33 (numbered 34): Prior Richard Teniesford	
	254	Ch.34:	Edward I
	254v	Ch.35:	Edward II
	254v	Ch.36:	Prior Robert Salle,1290
	255	Ch.37:	Edward II
	255	Ch.38:	Edward III, Edward II, Edward III
	255v	Ch.39:	Prior Thomas Warmington, verse.
		Ranulph Higden finishes his work: Strecche acknowledges his principal source.	
	256v	Ch.40:	Prior John Peyto,1344, verse
	257	Ch.41:	Prior Henry Bradewey,1361
	257v	Ch.42:	Edward III
	258	Ch.43:	....

	258	Ch.44:	....
	258v	Ch.45:	....
	259	Ch.46:	Richard II
	259v	Ch.47:	Prior Walter Charlton,1375
	259v	Ch.48:	Richard II
	260v	Ch.49:	....
	260v	Ch.50:	Henry Duke of Lancaster .
	261	Ch.51:	Richard II
	261v		verse (Catchword for e1)

262 BOOK FIVE, Part One, Henry IV

Qe1.	262	Ch. 1	Henry IV
	262	Ch. 2	....
	262v	Ch. 3	Prior Thomas Merston,1384
	263	Ch. 4	Prior Walter Brayles,1400
	263	Ch. 5	Henry IV
	263v	Ch. 6	....
	264	Ch. 7	....
	264	Ch. 8:	....
	264v	Ch. 9:	....
	264v	Ch.10:	....
	265	Ch.11:	Richard Scrope, Archbishop of York

265 BOOK FIVE, Part Two, Henry V

265 to 279v, 27 Chapters. These are given as a Latin
transcript, without translation, by Frank Taylor, 1932,
Bulletin of John Rylands Library.

Qf1. 269v, 270, form Chapter 10, Tombs and Images of the
Founders, with a verse giving the foundation of the
Priory as 1119. This is the only Chapter in Book 5,
Part 2, concerning Kenilworth Priory.

Qg3. 279v End of verse in praise of Henry V, and end of the
whole manuscript.

Primary Sources

Primary Source 1a. Thomas Morstede 'Fair Book of Surgery', 1420 - 1450, ed. R.Theodore Beck 1974 in 'The Cutting Edge', p.117. Originally published by Lund Humphries, now Ashgate Publishing, who have given approval for including this extract here, the editing author's permission having been sought.

And yt ys to undyrstond that in the yer of owr lorde M CCCC IIJ in the IIJ yer of kynge Herry the IIIJ on Mary Mawdlen Evyn at the batell of schrewesbery yt happyn soo that Herry the worthy prynce and eyr of the sayd Herry kynge was smetyn in the face besyd the nose on the lefte syd with an arow the wyche sayd arow entryd overwharte and after the schafte wase takyn owt and the hede ther of abod styll in the hyndrparte of a bone of the hede after the mesur of vj ynche and that was John Bradmore surgen to the kynge and helyd hym in the castell of Kelyngworth to the sayd castell come that tyme dyverse of wise lechys say and thet thei wolde draw owt the arrow hed with drynkys and odyr curis but thei myght not and at the laste the sayd John Bradmore entyr melynge of the sayd cur and had owt the arow hede wyth an Instrument mad in the maner of a tonges and was Rownde and holowysche & be the myddes ther of entryd a lytyll wyse with the wyche instrument was pullyd owt the arrow hed and afterward the wounde was wasched with wyne and clensyd with mundificatype onyment of iij parttes of populion and the iiij part of honey so contynewynge the space of vij dayes and afterward the place was helyd with unguentum fuscum cirurgicum

> lechys - physicians: popilion - see 1b:
> ung.fusc.cir. - surgeons' dark ointment, based on tallow and turpentine

Primary Source 1b. Anon.1443, MS136, Medical Society of London, ed. Dawson, Warren W. 1934. *A leechbook, or collection of medical recipes of the 15th century.* Macmillan, London, p.111.

289. For to make an entrete called popilion: Take four pounds of the young buds of poplars; of henbane, little morell, orpine, sengreen each one pound; of endive, violet, watercress each half a pound. Wash them clean and stamp them, and put thereto half a pound of boar's grease, molten and purified. When they are well mingled, put them into a pot, close it and let it stand nine days. Set it on the fire in a pan and stir well with a slice, that it stick not to the bottom. Strain it into a vessel, set it over the fire again, and put thereto half a quartern of wax and a quartern of wether's tallow and boil them a little. Then put thereto a quartern of incense powdered well and stir it well together till it be softened and relented. And then anon take it down and strain it, and let it cool. Cover it and let out the water, cleanse the underside of the scum and set it over the fire again till it be molten, and with a feather skim it. And this is the making of popilion kindly.

(All parts of black poplar are known to contain the anti-inflammatory substance salicin: information kindly supplied bv The Royal Pharmaceutical Society).

Primary Source 2. John Strecche, Add.MS 35295, fos.269v, 270. Transcription by F.Taylor[41]. (Translation pp.10,9)

De tumba et pictura fundatorum

Et eodem anno quarto Henrici regis quinti et incarnacionis domini
mccccxvii placuit Iohanni Mukelton tunc cellerario suppriori et
conventui toto quod de novo ornarent et depingerent tumbas
fundatorum in domo capellari prioratus de Kenilleworda. Set
remota tumba lignea que stetit super sepulcre dictorum fundatorum
tres lapides marmorei ibi apparuerunt ex quibus medium lapidem
de conventu quidam erexerunt sub quo Galfridus de Glintona in
redolenti poliandro integer quiescit. Quo viso et palpato dictum
lapidem super sargosagum ut prius fuerat collocarunt. Et dictam
tumbam cum ymaginibus fundatorum solempniter depinxerunt ut
ibidem palam possent intueri. De quibus huius operis compilator
metrice sic scripsit:

Anno milleno c bisque decem minus uno
Anglorum primus rex ens Henricus opimus
Tunc de Glintona Galfridus per pia dona
    Virginis in titulum condidit ecce locum
Condidit ecce locum matri Christi fore sacrum
Atque prioratum fundaverat hic sibi gratum
Canonicos voluit in eo Christo famulari
    Ast illis statuit munera cara dari
Munera cara dari miles statuit probitatis
Que rex firmari monuit motu pietatis.
Tunc nece preventus celestia tiro petivit
Quem flens conventus cum laudibus hic sepelivit.
Annis sic iacuit centum bis lustris duodenis
Set multis patuit membris sub marmore plenis
Nobilis Henrici regis modo tempore quinti
Anglorum quarto recte regnantis in anno
Cilicio tectus non est alius sibi lectus.
    In tumba redolet sordibus atque caret
Sordibus ille caret ut Christo sanctificatus
Integer ille manet in corpore non maculatus.
Filius atque nepos eius sunt tumulati.
Christi nunc sit honor et gloria lausque perhennis

Cuius fas et amor crescat in mente Johannis.
Peccantis misere deus alme mei miserere
Crimina condona multiplicaque bona. Amen.

'Primary Source' 3. Robert Browning, Dramatic Lyrics
Soliloquy of the Spanish Cloister, stanzas I, II, and VI of 9.

Grrr.. there goes my heart's abhorrence.
Water your damned flower pots, do.
If hate killed men, Brother Lawrence,
God's blood, would not mine kill you!
What? Your myrtle bush wants trimming?
Oh, that rose has prior claims -
Wants its leaden vase filled brimming -
Hell dry you up with its flames!

At the meal we sit together:
Salve tibi. I must hear
Wise talk of the kind of weather,
Sort of season, time of year:
Not a plenteous cork crop - scarcely
Dare we hope oak galls, I doubt.
What's the Latin name for parsley?
What's the Greek name for swine's snout!

Oh, those melons! If he's able
We're to have a feast - so nice!
One goes to the Abbot's table:
All of us get each a slice.
How go on your flowers? None double?
Not one fruit-sort can you spy?
Strange. And I, too, at such trouble
Keep them close-snipped on the sly.

Primary Source 4. The Fable of Albina from *Eulogium Historiarum*, possibly by Thomas of Malmesbury, ca.1366 (Rolls Series 9 ii, F.S.Haydon,ed.)

Anno a creatione mundi III.M.DCCCC erat in Graecia rex potentissimus, supra caeteros reges obtinens principatum: vir magnae staturae et similem habens uxorem, ex qua XXX filias magnae staturae genuerat, quas regibus maritavit, et senior vocabatur Albina: quae more feminarum singulae petulantes noluerunt maritis suis se subjici sed supra eis extolli: et super eo inter illas inito consilio ordinaverunt, per juramentum suum praestitum quod omnes una et eadem hora suos maritos interficerent, dum ipsae in salaciis et carnali coitu fuerant cum eisdem. sed earum junior, dominum suum diligens, huiusmodi ordinatis consentire noluit, sed tamen prae timore mortis contradicere non audebat: quo doloso facto consilio omnes ad propria redierunt. et illarum junior cum maritum suum vidisset, statim ab ejus oculis lacrymae erumpebant. cuius ploratus maritus inquirens causam ipsa veniam genuflectendo humiliter postulans sibi huiusmodi proditionem ordinatam narravit per ordinem et qualiter timore mortis sibi illatae occisione suae consenserat verbaliter et non corde. quo per maritum audito ipse uxorem suam in amplexibus osculatus est, dicens quod super hoc Deus apponeret remedium. Mane autem facto ipsi simul ad regem Graeciae accedentes retulerunt sibi omnia per ipsas filias suas tam proditionaliter ordinata, quod rex Graeciae moleste gerens statim direxit suas literas, annulo regis signatas, quod dicti reges cum suis uxoribus ad suum conspectum venirent. Quibus omnibus accersitis, dictis filiabus per patrem suum super his seorsum examinatis et subtiliter victis, filias suas capi et incarcerari mandavit, donec seniorum consilio et sapientum quid contra eos fiere deberet ad plenum deliberaretur in hac parte. Et licet ipsae vilissimam mortem propterea meruerant, quia tamen de tanti regis sanguine fuerant, idem rex adjudicavit eas mitti debere in exilium, juniore excepta: ordinans quod dictae filiae suae, absque remis, vehiculis, gubernatoribus, et cibariis, et potibus ponerentur in navibus, quod et factum est: unde dictae mulieres absque anchoris in nave sic positae, et in altum mare per undas et fluctus huc et

71

illuc miserabiliter deductae in magno periculo ponebantur, et fere fame et doloribus perierunt, cadentes saepius in extasim, tempestatibus undique conquassatae tribus diebus et noctibus: nullatenus se moventes postmodum, navis earum ad terram deducta est, et mari se retrahente Albina quae senior fuerat terram cepit, caeteris sororibus suis prae dolore in terram pronis jacentibus: resumptis viribus herbas crudas atque fructus arborum comederunt: reperientes terram Cornubiae absque habitatore, quam Albina suo nomine vocavit Albion. Terra autem huiusmodi feris et bestiis erat plena, de quibus ipsae mulieres comedere appetebant, sed ad capiendas eas, arma aliqua non habentes, subtiliter ordinaverunt quod de virgulis et vigiminibus virentibus fierent sibi trappas pro dictis bestiis capiendis, et eas cum petris a...tis de silice excoriantes, et in coreis earum carnes coquentes, sic ingeniose de silice ignem traxerunt et carnes coctas comederunt: taliter et pingues devenerunt, et cum tempore calore naturae abundaverunt statim de luxuria tentabantur, quod incubi considerantes cum oblectamentis coitus habuerant, tales incubi carnaliter coinstebant cum eis, neminem videntes sed spermata sentientes: sic quod dicti incubi ex eis gigantes horribiles genuerunt, et terram illam huiusmodi gigantibus repleverunt: qui totam terram occupantes et cum ad aetatem venerant ex matribus propriis filios et filias genuerunt, sibi in montibus cavernas subterraneas facientes, foveis profundis et muris contractis circumdederunt undique et muraverunt ibidem: ante Nativitatem Christi MCXXXVI annis. Britones denique terram illam per conquaestum habentes nomen Albion ex toto delentes terram Britanniae vocaverunt, et sic gigantes expulsi CXX annis terram Angliae tenuerunt in pace.

Primary Source 5. Castleton's Chronicle. This is a long verse history of England edited by Professor C.D.Eckhardt from the only known manuscript of about 1327 in the University library of Göttingen. 'Thomas Castleton' appears at the top of the first page but this is more likely to be the name of an owner of the manuscript than that of the author. The text is made available by kind permission of the Council of the Early English Text Society:

Here may men hear, all and some, how this land was first
named Albion:
In the noble land of Syria there was a noble king and mighty
And a man of great name then - men called him Dioclesian.
He him ruled full worthily, chief he was of chivalry
So that he conquered and won all the lands about him then.
And almost all the kings, moreover, in this world both far and near
To him were they almost all bound to come at his call.

Of Dioclesian it befell thus, that he would wive and have a
                            spouse,
A gentle damsel and a fair, that was his neighbour's daughter and
                            his heir.
Albana she was called, sooth to say, none fairer living in that day.
And with his wife he had soothly, daughters full fair, three and
                            thirty.
One of these daughters, fair and free, men called her dame Albina.
When these maidens come of age, that they would, and men
                            should, weld,
Their father full soon letters he sent to all the kings were at his
                            commandment.
And other lords should to him come, dukes and earls of their
                            kingdom,
A feast for to make royal as in letters declared more special.
And they come thither at that day and with them their lords in
                            royal array:
Many dukes and noble chivalry. The feast was arrayed full royally
And there they lived in mirth and bliss, enough there was of all
                            riches.
And up him stood then Dioclesian, and his language thus began:

That he thought among all those kings to marry his daughters,
                    his darlings.
And they went together then that richly were married those women
Unto three and thirty kings: married were all those fair maidens.
And when ended was this solemnity, each king went to his
                    own country,
And with them took they their wives, rich queens to be in their
                    estates.

And afterward, it was well seen, dame Albina became so
                    stubborn and keen
That little praise of her husband she told and would naught do but
                    as she would.
She had of him scorn and despite and full oft with him would she
                    fight.
And ill manners many on. And all her sisters, every one,
Bore them so evil against their lords that they had wonder of their
                    discords. ....
But the kings that were their lords would have chastised them with
                    fair words
And bequests and gifts as well, and warned them in fair manner
Upon all friendship they should amend and their scornful
                    conditions bryng to end.
But all it was for nought to say: they followed their own wills
                    alway.
Wherefore the kings their wives threatened and oftentymes they
                    them beat ....
But of such conditions they are .. that for fair speech and for
                    warning
They did their worst in all kind of thing .. their ill conditions might
                    no man guess
Wherefore the king that Albina wed wrote of the ill conditions
                    and the wrongs
Of his wife dame Albina then, and the letter sent to Dioclesiane.
And when the other kings heard how the lord of Albina fared,
Letters anon they sent forth all, sealed with their seals most
                    principal.

Ah! When Dioclesiane those letters had read, his daughters
conditions, how they fared,
He was ashamed and fell as fire towards his daughters so full of ire.
He thought him both day and night he would amend them if he
might.
Their sore misdeeds he was ashamed of and send forth letters
thereupon
Unto those kings three and thirty they should not tarry but come
in haste
And bring with them their wives all: he would them chastise
whatso befall
For there he would them chastise soon, their wickedness they so
misdone.
So all the kings come at the day that time was set without delay ....
The king made a feast with much worship unto all were under his
lordship.
The third day of that solemnity he sent for his daughters thirty
three
That they should come to his chamber to speak with him of things
sere.
And when they were come therein, he spake to them with
words grim:
He blamed them of their wickedness, their cruelty and their
spitefulness.
He them reproved, all and some, their wickedness and their evil
custom.
He warned them to amend, therefore, or they should his love lose
for evermore.
And all those ladies move and was greatly ashamed of their
reproof.
And to their father all they say, they would amend in that they
may.
Their father's chamber they parted from. Dame Albina then was
full thrall.
The eldest sister of them all, into her chamber she called them all.
She made void all that therein was, so that her sisters to counsel
goes.

Then said to her sisters Dame Albina 'Our father has us reputed shamefully,
Despised us, with great words fell. The cause is, ye know full well,
To make us obedient our husbands to. But certain that shall I never do
Seeing I am of king's blood, higher than my husband is, be feared!
He will alway enough be my servant, to hold me waiter to my hand.'
And when her tale was told, her sisters thought she had said well
And all the sisters vowed they would never obey their husbands' will.
Then said Albina to them everyone 'Our husbands have us complained upon.
Wherefore, sisters, my counsel keep: when our husbands are in bed asleep,
We all with one assent then cut the throats of every man.
And then we may be in peace of them and go where we will without claim.
And better we may do this here under our father's power than elsewhere.'
Anon all these ladies, with one will, consent to this ill counsel.
And when they were in bed asleep, those lords, they cutted all their husbands' throats!

And so they have their husbands slain: great sorrow made all men certain.
And when that Dioclesiane, the king, had heard of his daughters' doing
He against them all became full wrath and would have burnt them, hide and cloth,
But that the lords of Syria soon counselled him not so for to do
Unto his daughters so cruel a deed, but would them banish out of that sted
So that they never again come, and thus it was his lordes doom.
Anon their father, with little moan, commanded them to board a ship every one,

And gave them victuals for half a year. They left their friends to
their gods dear.
So, long they sailed on the sea, till they came to an island,
soothly.
This isle was all wilderness that to come were all the sisters.
Albina first the land has take and said to her sisters 'For my sake
Because I am eldest of you all and first on land my foot has fall,
I will, after my name Albina, Albion be called this country.'
And all her sisters with good will granted her her asking still.
To land went those sisters, all and some, named after their sister
'Albion'.
They went on all sides and they found up and down nothing living:
Man nor woman, wife nor child, but all the land it was full wild.
Beasts of divers kinds truly were inhabiting all the country.
And when dispensed was their vital, with herbs and fruits they fed
tham all
And lived as they might do best, and took the flesh of divers beasts,
And became in likeness wondrous fat. Men's company desired
they after that,
That they desired more company of men than other mirth or solace.

When the Devil perceived all this, he went by many divers
countries
And took body of the air he had and like the natures of men
appeared,
And come to the land of Albion and lay by those women, all and
some,
And shed those natures upon them and they consented to the same.
And after, giants they brought forth there. Gogmagog one of them
were,
Langrygane hight another: many divers names had all they together.
Thus they multiplied all these lands and were in Albion horrible
giants.
In Albion they dwelt in caves and hills and all the land at their wills,
Unto the time that Brutus arrived at Totnes and out them drived,
And discomfort those giants and won the realm into his hands.

———————————

REFERENCES

References to 'in *Kenilworth History*' are to the annual magazine published by the Kenilworth History and Archaeology Society, available in Kenilworth Public Library.

The Rolls Series was a Victorian Government initiative to make medieval manuscripts widely available, in transcription, and sometimes translation. The volumes are in Warwick University Library and Birmingham Reference Library.

As a concession to 21st century culture, three of the titles here have been nominated for the Award of 'Most Astonishing Medieval Good Read'.

Folio numbers in the two manuscripts by Strecche are in a separate list at the end of these references, in the order in which they occur in the text, signified by chapter and phrase.

1. Arnold, T. 1879. *Henrici Archidiaconi Huntendunensis, Historia Anglorum.* Rolls Series 54, London.
2. Beck, R.Theodore. 1974. *The Cutting Edge: early history of the surgeons of London.* Lund Humphries, London.p.117
3. Bottomley, F. 1995. *The Abbey Explorer's Guide.* Smith Settle, London. p.196. (Chapter 9 heading, quotation from Webster's *Duchess of Malfi.*
4. Brereton, G. 1978. *Froissart: Chronicles.* Penguin Classics. pp.48-50. 'Astonishing Read' runner-up.
5. British Library, London, catalogue of manuscripts website: //molcat.bl.uk/msscat/ has Descriptions of Additional Manuscripts 35295 and 38665 by John Strecche, and 47677, fo.X,Henry III.
6. Brown, M.P. 1993. *A guide to western historical scripts from antiquity to 1600.* The British Library, London. p.100-101
7. Browning, R. 1842. *Dramatic Lyrics.* Chapter 3. heading, quotation from Soliloquy of the Spanish Cloister.
8. Clarke, J.W. 1897. *Observances in use at the Augustinian Priory of Barnwell, Cambridge.* Macmillan and Bowes, Cambridge.

9. de Hamel, C. 2001. *The British Library Guide to Manuscript Illumination*. British Library, London.p.44

10. Drayton, M. ca.1590. *Polyolbion*. (web search)

11. Eckhardt, C.D.ed.1996. *Castleford's Chronicle or the Boke of Brut*. Early English Text Society, O.U.P. pp.i,1-7

12. Fournier, S. 1998. *A brief history of parchment*. Les éditions Fragile, Gavaudun, France.

13. Galbraith, V.H. 1930. The deposition of Richard II. *Bulletin of the John Rylands University Library,Manchester*.14.pp180-1

14. Gransden, A. 1982. *Historical writing in England, vol.ii, ca.* in *1307- early Sixteenth Century*. Routledge and Kegan Paul, London. pp.322,343,408

15. Greenway, D. 2002. *Henry of Huntingdon, The history of the English people 1000-1154*. Oxford World Classics. pp.4,27,119. Latin from Rolls Series 54. 'Most Astonishing Medieval Good Read' Award Winner.

16. Guyot de Provens, ca.1250 A.D. Chapter 1 heading, quotation

17. Gwynn, David. Personal communication.

18. H.M.S.O. 1904. Calendar of Inquisitions, Henry III, p.149

19. Hardy, W.ed. 1864. *Jehan de Wavrin, Chroniques et Anchiennes Istoires de la Grant Bretaigne*. Rolls Series 39 i, London. pp.6-35

20. Haydon F.S.ed. 1860. *Eulogium Historiarum*. Rolls Series 9ii, London. pp.216-18

21. Hearne, T.ed. 1745. *Historia regum Angliae Johannis Rossi*.

22. Hilton, G.M. 2003. *A Portrait of Kenilworth in Street-Names, 2nd edition*. G.M.Hilton, Kenilworth. p.42

23. Hilton, G.M. 2003. Chronicle of John Strecche. *Bulletin of The John Rylands University Library, Manchester*. Vol.85(1).

24. Hilton, G .M. and Jackson, B.D.L. 2001. *The chronicle of John Strecche* in Kenilworth History 2001-2002. Kenilworth History and Archaeology Society. pp.18-21

25. Hodgetts, C. and Hill, S. 2000. Progress Report. in *Kenilworth History 2000-2001*. Kenilworth History and Archaeology Society, Kenilworth. pp.3-6

26. Ivy, G.S. 1958. The bibliography of the manuscript book in *The English library before 1700*. Wormald, F. and Wright, C.E.,eds. University of London.

27. Jackson, B.D.L. 1993. Chaucer, Gaunt and the Church: a speculation. in *Kenilworth History 1993*. pp.17-18.

28. Jackson, B.D.L. 2000. Historical evidence for the de Clinton burials. in *Kenilworth History 2000-2001*. pp.19-20.

29. Jackson, B.D.L. 2000. Anyone for tennis? in *Kenilworth History, 2000-2001*. pp.27-9

30. Kenilworth Abbey Interpretation Scheme 2003. *The Abbey of St Mary, Kenilworth*. (Free leaflet) Warwick District Council, Warwick. www.kenilworthabbey.org

31. Ker, N. 1953. Medieval manuscripts from Norwich Cathedral Priory. *Transactions of the Cambridge Bibliographical Society I*. p.9.

32. Kingsford, C.L. 1913. *English Historical Literature in the Fifteenth Century*. Oxford. pp.39-43

33. Lumby, J.R.ed. 1882. *Polychronicon Ranulphi Higden Monarchi Cestrensis, with English translations of John Trevisa and unknown 15th century author*. Rolls Series 41, vii,viii. London. pp.7-8

34. Sherley-Price, L. 1968. *Bede, A history of the English church and people*. Penguin Classics. 'Astonishing Read' Runner-up

35. Spenser, Edmund 1590. *The Faerie Queene*. Stanza VIII. (Chapter 5 heading)

36. Stanton,J.M. 1969. *Agricultural Records, A.D.220-1968*. John Baker, London.

37. Stephenson,J.ed. 1854. *William of Malmesbury: the Kings before the Norman Conquest*. Reprint 1989 by Llanerch Press, Lampeter, Wales.

38. Sunley, H. 1997. *Problems at Brooke* in Kenilworth History 1997-1998. K.H.A.S.

39. Sunley, Harry. Personal communication.

40. Sunley, H.L.G. and Stevens,N.W. 1995. *Kenilworth, the story of the Abbey*. Pleasaunce Press, Kenilworth. pp.34b,72a,10a,22a

41. Taylor, F. 1932. The chronicle of John Strecche for the reign of Henry V. *Bulletin of the John Rylands Library*. Manchester. pp.137-87,143-145

42. Thomson, R.M. 1989. *Catalogue of the manuscripts of Lincoln Cathedral chapter library*. Brewer, London.

43. Thorpe, L. 1966. *Geoffrey of Monmouth, The history of the kings of Britain.* Penguin Classics. pp.54-73,284. (Chapter 4 heading)

44. Victoria History of the Counties of England 1949. *Volume 5, Warwick.* Oxford University Press. 90b-92

45. Wilson, R.M. 1940. The medieval library of Titchfield Abbey. *Proceedings of Leeds Philosophical and Literary Society*, V. Leeds. pp.150-276

46. Winkless, D. 1990. *Hailes, the story of a Gloucestershire abbey.* Spridden Press, Stockfield, Northumberland.(Chapter 2 heading, words of St Bernard, plaque on north cloister wall)

List of folio numbers cited in text:

MS 35295, unless stated as MS 38665:

Chapter One

cheerfully careless box   fo.136v

penitent colophon   38665 fo.55

devotional end to poem   fo.270

student drawn his master   38665 fo.87v

words of the acrostic on the title page   fo.2v

verses announced with a flourish   fo.249, fo.261v

the burial of Prior Robert Salle   fo.255

preclude study, as would the Saint's day marked   fo.5

Henry was treated after the Battle of Shrewsbury   fo.263v

and at least four more occasions at *castellum*   fo.278

Chapter Three

Strecche records lending books to 'dominus'   38665 fo.168v

the following eulogy for Edward II   fo.255 (Higden vol.8, p.324)

short chapter on Richard I he selects   fo.249 (Higden vol.8, p.82)

indirectly acknowledges debt to Ranulph Higden fo.255v **Fig.10a**

cannot resist tale against William   fo.247v (Higden vol.7, p.314)

Deposition of Richard II in a passage ending   fo.263v **Fig.10c**

'immense stature' but Strecche merely says 'a giant'   fo.240v

Chapter Four

Geoffrey's work faithfully, including copyright warning   fo.228v

complains that Troy was only conquered by trickery   fo.136v

Chapter Five

Sisters you are most noble *O sorores et domine nobillissime* fo.230,line 31

slew their husbands while drugged *leti fero dolo intoxicata* fo.230v,line 27

A boat was brought to the shore *ratis quidem in ripa sualis sine remige* fo.231,line 17

search for fruit from the trees *aliis arborum fructibusque vestobantur* fo.231v,line 1

and from them they gave birth to giants *et ex eis gygantes generunt* fo.231v,line 13

My advice is confirmed *iam appello ad philosophum Theofrastum* fo.232,line 2 **Fig.10b**

Chapter Six

he has to write round fo.231

you have desired this work from me fo.2v

death of Owen Gyndwr fo.264v

burial of Thomas Duke of Clarence fo.278v

copied out this poem himself 38665 fo.92v

Chapter Eight

Prior William de Evesham fo.253v **Fig.10d**

Chapter Nine

From the manuscript Dr Hodgetts identified fo.255

———————————————

Any enquiry about visits to The Barn Museum and the Abbey Site, should be made in the first place to the Author (who at the time of writing is Hon.Secretary of the Kenilworth History and Archaeology Society) or in the second place to Kenilworth Library, which keeps a record of the current Secretary of the Society.

———————————————

Text acknowledgements

Chapter One
Much of this chapter has appeared as an article by the author in the Bulletin of the John Rylands University Library of Manchester and is printed here by kind permission of the Editor.

Chapter Three
The extract from Froissart, reference 4, by G.Brereton is included by permission from Penguin Books Ltd. and the extract from Henry of Huntingdon, reference 15, by D. Greenway is included by permission from Oxford University Press.

Chapter Four
The extract from Geoffrey of Monmouth, reference 43, by L. Thorpe is included by permission from Penguin Books Ltd.

Chapter Eight
This chapter has appeared as an article by the author in *Kenilworth History 2003-4* and is printed here by kind permission of the Editor.

Figure 2b caption
The estimated purchasing power of medieval coins is by Medieval Re-enactors Ecorcheur Online.

INDEX

INDEX

About this book

The book sets the scene of the Medieval world through the eyes of a canon of Kenilworth Priory, writing for his students in 1420 A.D.

It examines his beliefs, piety and prejudices by reference to his own surviving manuscripts and to the legends in the history textbooks he read.

The book repeoples the scant remains of Kenilworth Abbey and indeed of more than 800 ruined abbeys throughout the British Isles built to a similar plan.

While appealing to the general reader and to residents of Kenilworth, and its visitors, it is fully referenced and will be of value to students of history, who will find many of the author's researches have not been published before.

The Primary Sources section includes extracts from texts not easily available, such as Morested's 'Fair Book of Surgery' and the quaintly poetic Castleton's Chronicle. Here, and in the main text, there are examples of middle English, old French, and Latin, usually translated, but with an element of challenge to the reader.

The author taught in Schools and the University of Wolverhampton. He is Hon.Secretary of Kenilworth History and Archaeology Society and has published 'A Portrait of Kenilworth in Street-Names', now in its second edition.
